Teaching Global Literacy Using Mnemonics

Teaching Global Literacy Using Mnemonics

Joan Ebbesmeyer

with illustrations by Brent Morris

Teacher Ideas Press, an imprint of Libraries Unlimited
Westport, Connecticut • London

Library of Congress Cataloging-in-Publication Data

Ebbesmeyer, Joan.
  Teaching global literacy using mnemonics / by Joan Ebbesmeyer ; with illustrations by Brent Morris.
    p. cm.
  Includes bibliographical references and index.
  ISBN 1-59158-361-6 (pbk. : alk. paper)
  1. Geography—Study and teaching. 2. Geography—Study and teaching—
Activity programs. 3. Mnemonics. I. Title.
G73.E143 2006
910.71—dc22   2006023743

British Library Cataloguing in Publication Data is available.

Copyright © 2006 by Joan Ebbesmeyer

All rights reserved. No part of this book may be reproduced
in any form or by any electronic or mechanical means, including
information storage and retrieval systems, without permission in
writing from the publisher, except by a reviewer, who may quote brief
passages in a review. Reproducible pages may be copied for classroom
and educational programs only.

Library of Congress Catalog Card Number: 2006023743
ISBN: 1-59158-361-6

First published in 2006

Libraries Unlimited/Teacher Ideas Press, 88 Post Road West, Westport, CT 06881
A Member of the Greenwood Publishing Group, Inc.
www.lu.com

Printed in the United States of America

The paper used in this book complies with the
Permanent Paper Standard issued by the National
Information Standards Organization (Z39.48–1984).

10 9 8 7 6 5 4 3 2 1

Contents

Introduction vii

Chapter 1—United States of America 1

Chapter 2—Central America and Mexico 45

Chapter 3—Canada 59

Chapter 4—South America 75

Chapter 5—Europe 89

Chapter 6—Africa 105

Chapter 7—Australia and Oceania 119

Chapter 8—Antarctica 131

Chapter 9—Asia 145

    Index 159

Introduction

In an effort to make students aware of the world in which they live, an emphasis has recently been placed on global education. Educators have seen the need for a deeper understanding of the interdependence of peoples and nations around the world. We are in a critical and pivotal era of history. In our age of outstanding technical development, we have the opportunity to solve some of the desperate problems that confront us. Some of the most pressing problems include war, poverty, and terrorism. September 11, 2001, taught us that there is no place to hide and no solution that does not involve all nations of the world.

Today's students will be challenged in the future to find answers for questions of defense, food supplies, population control, disarmament, and terrorism. Their involvement—or lack of it—will have an impact the future of the world. A globally informed citizenry understands the relevance of the old axiom, "United we stand, divided we fall."

Educators realize they have a responsibility to provide sufficient and accurate information about the peoples and nations of the world. It begins with very young students learning about families and communities in different places and cultures throughout the world. Older students will gain new insights and perspectives as they learn about relationships and the interdependence of peoples across the globe. To gain that global perspective, students must be led to an awareness of the commonalities and connections of all humankind and to the necessity of solving world problems. Only with that understanding is there hope for an end to famine, hatred, and war.

What better way to excite students in the study of people and places around the world than through storytelling, activities in language arts (reading, writing, speaking), and the use of mnemonics?

Students are often confused about the locations of countries, states, and provinces. Mnemonics can help in learning and retention through the use of a fun story and a simple sentence. Sometimes it's done with a picture or rhyme. We're all familiar with picturing an athlete springing forward then falling back, to know what to do with your clock at daylight savings time. "Thirty days hath September, April, June, and November" is the rhyme that helps us remember the number of days in each month.

With the help of mnemonic stories, teachers can interest students in learning and retaining names of foreign places, as well as learning about the people who live in those places and many facts concerning their history and culture. Students will find it easier to remember names, locations, and facts when they are connected to a story or rhyme, and this may also lead to an expansion into other areas of the curriculum and inspire students to create mnemonics of their own.

Goals and Objectives

The suggested readings, maps, activities, and mnemonic stories will assist teachers in meeting the following goals and objectives:

1. To deepen the understanding of a global world and to develop respect for cultural differences
2. To provide a fun way, with storytelling and mnemonics, to learn the locations of countries, states, provinces, and other important global facts
3. To instill empathy for the common needs of all humankind
4. To apply critical and creative thinking skills to the solution of world problems
5. To strengthen reading and critical thinking skills by researching, organizing, and reporting information

Rationale

Global studies should, and can, be an exciting segment of the curriculum. What could be more fascinating than to learn about the planet on which we live? This includes the mysterious parts of Africa; the exotic countries of Asia and Australia; the fascinating nations of Europe with its long and historic past; the cold, endless lands of the Arctic; the vast stretches of South America; and our own awesome North America.

Unfortunately, many students find little interest or joy in global studies (geography) and evidently do not retain what they are taught during their school years. This is evidenced in the ignorance many adults display when questioned about the countries and cultures of our world. Many have little knowledge of even our close neighbors, Canada and Mexico.

Students may have a problem with learning and retaining global facts because of a lack of prior knowledge. Most students have little experience with strange new names of countries, cultures, and faraway locations. They need a familiar base of knowledge to connect to their new experiences. Teachers must find an association or connection with something students can understand. This association should be one that provides an emotional spark—curiosity, awe, love, compassion, anger or a combination of these to bring about the desire to learn more!

Stories, poems, tall tales, myths, rhymes, and fables can lead to the desired outcome.

It's called mnemonics!

Many colorful and enticing picture books can be used as an introduction. Go around the world with books and excellent stories representing other countries and cultures. Students can be part of the process by researching all the literature that can be found on the region that is being studied.

In some instances, the teachers may need to create stories of their own to help student retention through mnemonics and to serve as a model for students who might want to add to the originality of story writing and find fun in creating their own mnemonics.

Once the student has read or listened to stories of the exotic animals and surroundings of the rain forest, he or she may be motivated to learn more about a particular region of the world. The teacher is responsible for finding an interesting way to present locations, divisions, history, and the culture of countries and continents.

Too often the students are introduced to a lot of information before learning the *basics* of the region. The first things learned should be the states, provinces, territories, and countries of the world, and *precisely* where they are located. The use of mnemonics is an interesting way of doing this. After learning the basics of a region, the student can web into a natural progression of information concerning the place of study.

One way to teach locations is through mnemonics within a story. The story should be connected in some way with the facts to be learned. As noted earlier, teachers may need to create their own stories, myths, or rhymes in some instances and endeavor to include as much information as possible in the mnemonic. All the stories in this resource are examples of this method.

Connections to the National Geography Standards

The activities in this book are all connected to one or more of the U.S. National Geography Standards. These eighteen standards are divided into six groups:

1. The first group consists of three standards dealing with the use of maps, tools, and technology to analyze and report on **the world in spatial terms.**

2. The second group includes three standards that address the physical and human characteristics of Earth's regions and how cultures influence the perceptions of different **places and regions.**

3. The third group of two standards are concerned with the patterns and ecosystems of Earth, made up by the **physical systems.**

4. Group 4 includes five standards dealing with human population, cultures' economic interdependence, and cooperation and conflict among peoples, which influence **the human system.**

5. Group five consists of three standards focusing on human actions, physical systems, and the importance of resources affecting **the environment and society.**

6. The last group has two standards centering on interpreting the past, present, and planning for the future through **the use of geography.**

Description of U.S. Geography Standards

1. Use of maps and other geographical tools to gain and report information
2. How to organize information mentally about people, places, and localities in a spatial circumstance
3. How to classify the spatial organization of Earth's people, places, and localities
4. Human and physical characteristics found in Earth's regions
5. Explaining Earth's complexity and the localities created by people
6. Human perceptions of localities are influenced by culture and experience
7. Patterns of Earth's surface and how it is shaped by physical processes
8. Earth's ecosystems—their characteristics and spatial distribution
9. Arrangements, characteristics, and movements on Earth's surface and its human population
10. How Earth's cultural combinations are formed, explained, and arranged
11. Complexities of Earth's economic interdependence

12. Changes and patterns of human settlement and effects of human utilization of the planet
13. How Earth's people, through cooperation and conflict, can influence the arrangement and control of Earth's surface
14. How the actions of humans change the physical environment
15. How human systems are affected by physical systems
16. Resources and changes that occur because of use and distribution
17. How to explain the past through the application of geography
18. How to explain the present and plan for the future through the application of geography.

The national standards have been included as appropriate on the regional student activity sheets. This provides an opportunity for teachers to stay abreast of the standards' connection to the various units of study. It also provides a way to make students aware of the standards and of their importance.

TRAVELING THE WORLD WITH MNEMONICS

"New-mon-icks"—what a strange word! It comes from the name of the Greek goddess of memory, Mnemosyne, and means "mindful."

Sometimes our MINDS are so FULL of new information that it is hard to remember it all. So . . .

<blockquote>
When your brain is saying NIX!
Why not try MNEMONIC TRICKS?
</blockquote>

Anything is easier to remember if you connect it with a story, a picture, a sentence, or a rhyme.

"Thirty days hath September, April, June and November" is a rhyme mnemonic that helps us remember the number of days in each month.

Remembering the names of states, provinces, and countries can be difficult. With the help of mnemonics, you can travel and learn the world without packing. You'll know where you are going and where you have been!

All it takes is a fun story and a simple sentence.

Chapter 1

United States of America

The United States of America

A good way to begin learning about the world is to start with our own country, the United States of America!

The program should start in kindergarten, and the country could take a lifetime of study as we become more knowledgeable about this great land that stretches from Canada to Mexico and from the Atlantic Ocean to the Pacific. Remembering what we know about these fifty states can be a daunting task!

Mnemonics can be a great help.

As explained in the Introduction, a mnemonic is anything that assists one's memory. A story, rhyme, or silly sentence can help students remember facts that would otherwise slip from their memories. Learning and remembering the locations and important facts about the fifty states can be difficult, but its importance demands we find ways to get students interested and excited in the endeavor. There are many books and poems about our country to motivate a student's interest in learning more. The ones listed here, and many others, can lead to an interest in the mnemonics chosen for the United States.

It will be a puzzle!

Students can learn in many fun and creative ways where the puzzle pieces fit and how to remember them.

After reading a story, book, or poem to motivate interest (see Suggested Reading that follows), the map, as well as the state puzzle pieces, on the following pages can be reproduced and enlarged. Students can learn to place the states in the correct locations with the help of the activities.

It can be a class project with a large map displayed in the classroom, as well as an individual endeavor if all students have their own maps.

Suggested Reading

Picture Books

Johnson, Angela. *Those Building Men.* Illustrated by Barry Moser. Blue Sky Press, 2001.
> Building railroads, canals, skyscrapers, roads, and bridges is an exciting thing to think about. It is all wonderfully illustrated in this book, which brings the story of the toil and sacrifice that the builders of early America endured to create our modern country. Young students can be lead to understand the value of our multicultural heritage through the pictures and ideas in the words of this book.

Nikola-Lisa, W. *America: My Land, Your Land, Our Land.* Lee & Low Books, 1999.
> The America of this beautifully illustrated picture book for young students is ideal for showing the contrasts of this great land. Students will see the hot and cold, the rich and poor, the bright and dark, the low and high, the wetlands and the dry of the United States. The pictures can lead to many informative discussions on the locations of the fifty states and their wonderful diversity.

Poetry

Siebert, Diane. *Heartland* (1992). *Mississippi* (2001). *Mojave* (1992). *Sierra* (1995). HarperCollins Publishers.

These four poetry books, written by Diane Siebert, describe in rhymed form all of the land regions of the forty-eight contiguous states. These books are a treasure trove of information about the people, history, weather, ecosystems and culture of the many areas that make up this vast country. Like Whitman's "I Hear America Singing," these books are also an inspiration for creative writing. (See the activities that follow for ways to use these books.)

Whitman, Walt. *I Hear America Singing*. Illustrated by Robert Sabuda. Philomel Books, 1991.

Whitman's poem from *Leaves of Grass* is a classic piece and unrhymed tribute to the workers of America. This picturebook of the poem is bright and colorful and can be used to motivate students to research and write pattern-poems on other aspects of America. (See the activity "I Hear America Singing" later in this chapter.)

Chapter Books

Schlein, Mirium. *I Sailed with Columbus*. Illustrated by Tom Newsom. HarperCollins, 1991.

This chapter book is written as though by a twelve-year-old boy and starts with the adventures of Christopher Columbus, the explorer who didn't know he had discovered a new world. The book is in the form of a diary and tells the day-by-day happenings on Christopher Columbus's flagship, the *Santa Maria*.

Julio is chosen to serve as ship's boy on the most exciting sailing expedition that has ever been planned. He cannot resist the idea of experiencing the adventures that await him on the unknown sea. He realizes there will also be many dangers as the group sails so many miles on uncharted seas. But Julio knows he cannot give up this chance of a lifetime!

The book is filled with many exciting and life-threatening encounters, and Julio faithfully recounts each one in his daily journal. The text will also teach students about the West Indies, islands to the south east of Florida.

4 Teaching Global Literacy Using Mnemonics

United States Activities: Mapmaking

Make a Map (Standards 1 and 2)

There should be a large map of the United States in one area of the classroom. All states should be outlined but not labeled. Alaska is outlined above the map and Hawaii to the left side. Inform students that the "Map Puzzle" will be solved as clues are provided on the following pages. The map below can be reproduced and enlarged.

Sample of large map of the United States of America.

Each student should have a smaller copy of this map to complete as the activities progress. Encourage students to name any states they know but not to fill in the states by copying from a labeled map. Provide a thin sheet of tracing paper to enable students to become familiar with the configuration of the states.

The following maps and activities will allow students to fill in their puzzle pieces as the study progresses over the days, weeks, and months. These activities can be expanded with additional teacher and student mnemonic ideas and can be incorporated into the entire curriculum with connections to science, math, social studies, and language arts.

Place Puzzles (Standards 1, 2, and 7)

1. Allow students to work in pairs or groups to cut, fit, and paste the puzzle pieces (located on the following pages) to their maps. A large piece of tag board should be supplied to each student. Each puzzle piece has a written clue (supplied later in the chapter) to help students discover the correct state name and its location. Observing configurations will help in learning and retention.

2. Rather than overwhelming young students with all fifty state pieces at once, consider working in sections and using a mnemonic to evoke interest. There are additional activity ideas throughout this chapter, numbered 2 through 5, offering ways to identify the different states.

3. Because a mnemonic is anything that aids memory and evoking an emotion aids learning and retention, poems and stories of excellence can serve as great mnemonic connections to the many U.S. states, as well as to other countries of the world. Some book ideas and suggestions are found on pages 2 and 3. Many more can be found in the library.

The pages of clues (found at the end of this chapter) can be handed out to each student, or each clue could be pasted on the individual puzzle pieces to aid in determining the state locations.

State Puzzle Pieces

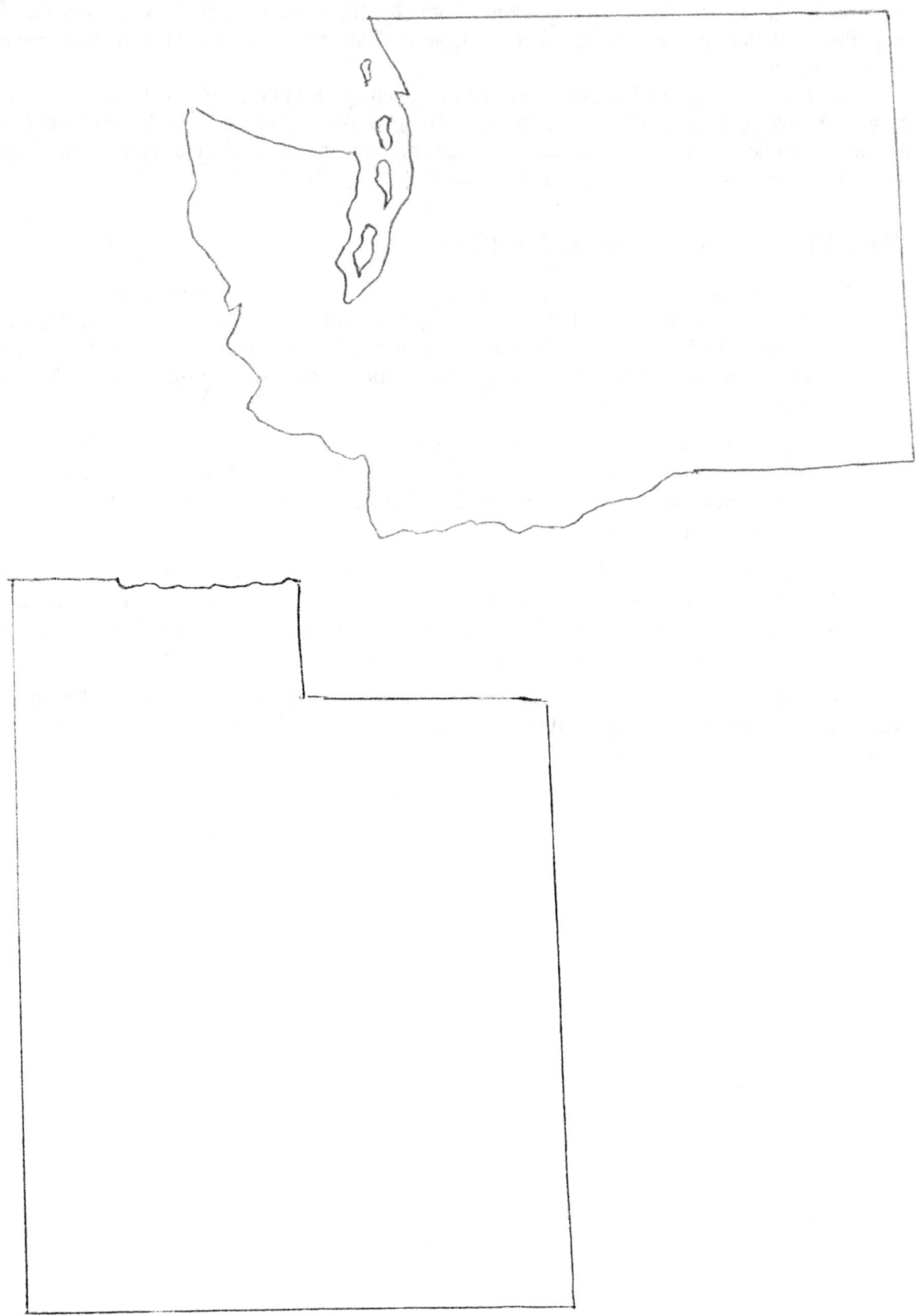

From *Teaching Global Literacy Using Mnemonics* by Joan Ebbesmeyer.
Westport, CT: Libraries Unlimited/Teacher Ideas Press. Copyright © 2006.

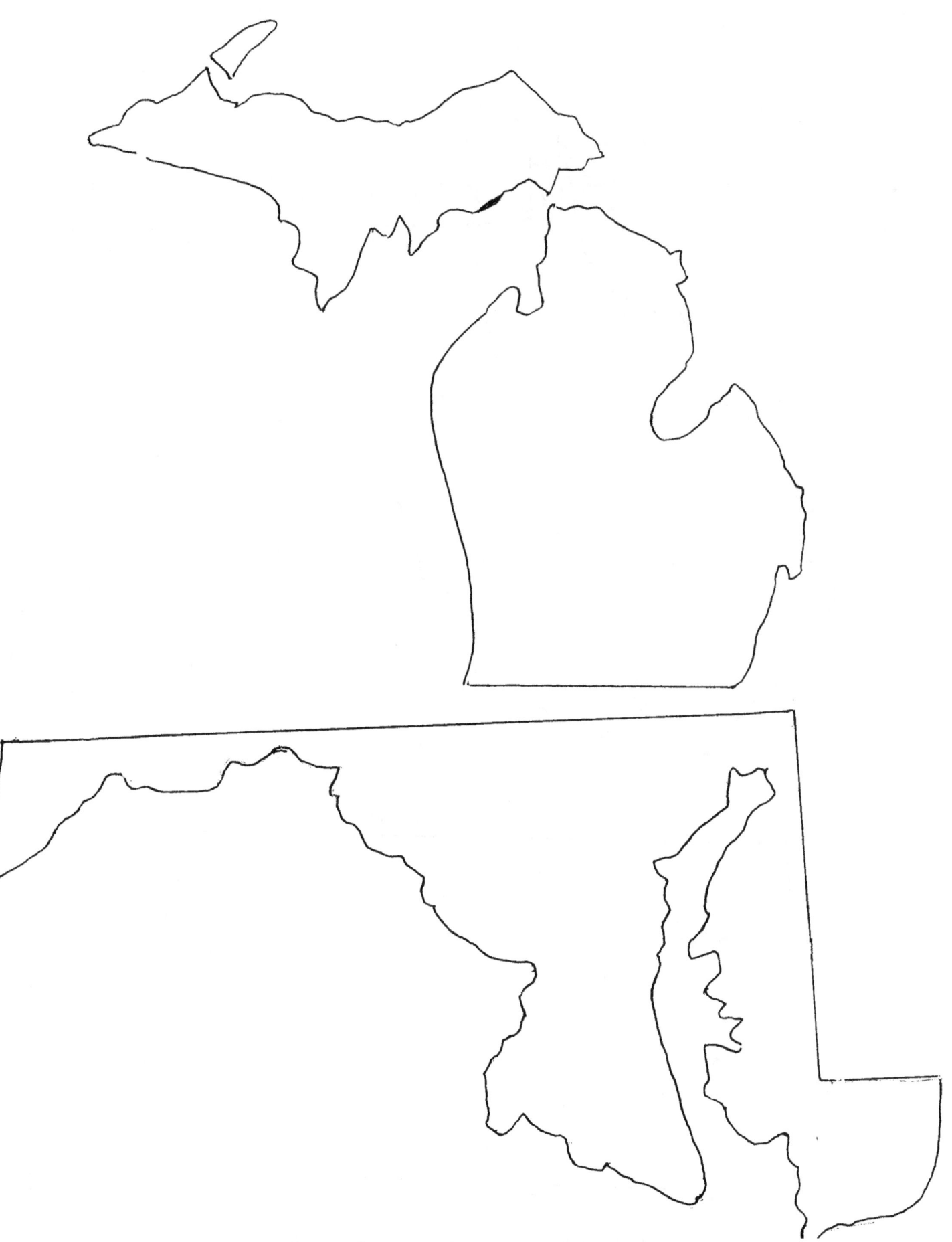

From *Teaching Global Literacy Using Mnemonics* by Joan Ebbesmeyer.
Westport, CT: Libraries Unlimited/Teacher Ideas Press. Copyright © 2006.

From *Teaching Global Literacy Using Mnemonics* by Joan Ebbesmeyer.
Westport, CT: Libraries Unlimited/Teacher Ideas Press. Copyright © 2006.

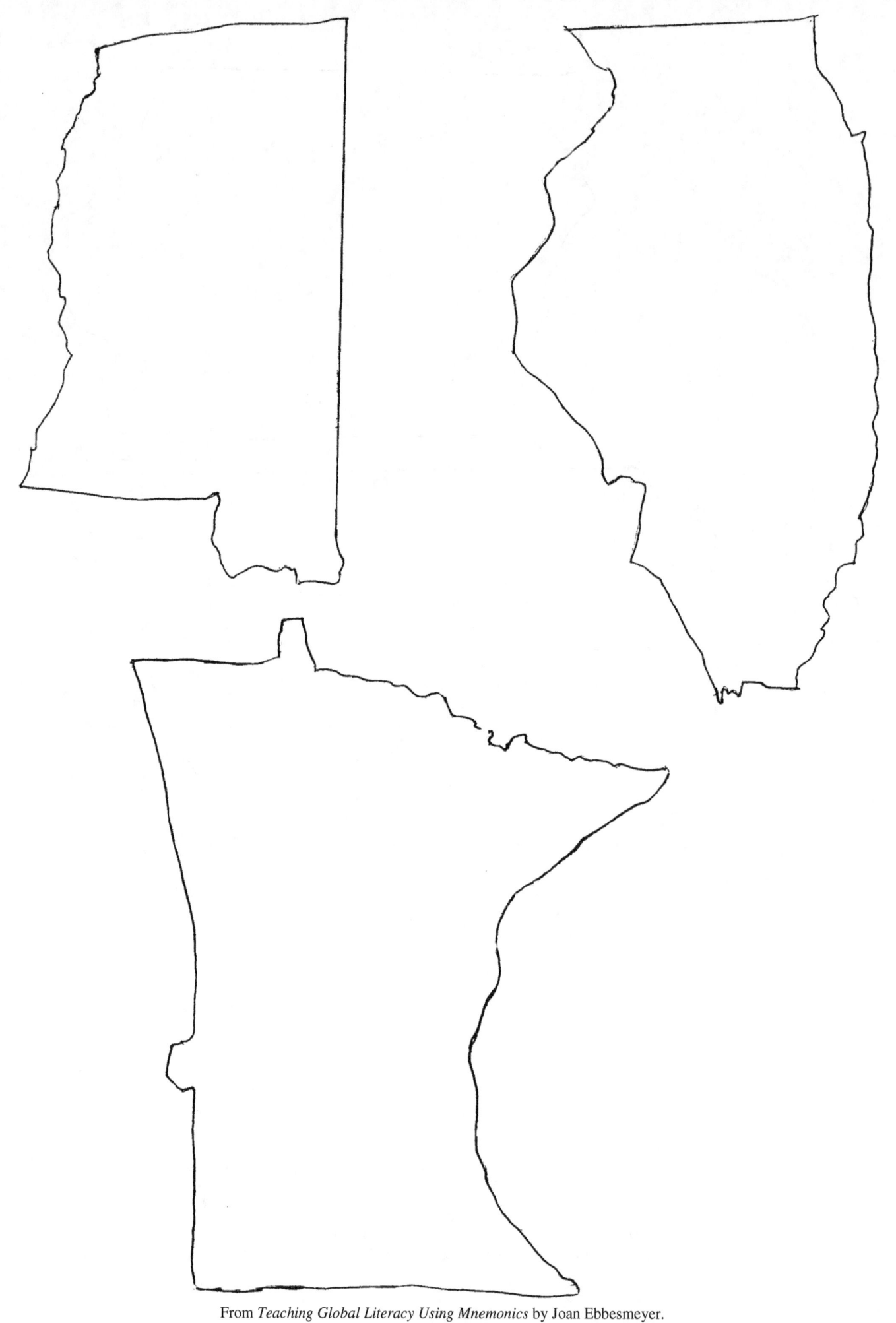

From *Teaching Global Literacy Using Mnemonics* by Joan Ebbesmeyer.
Westport, CT: Libraries Unlimited/Teacher Ideas Press. Copyright © 2006.

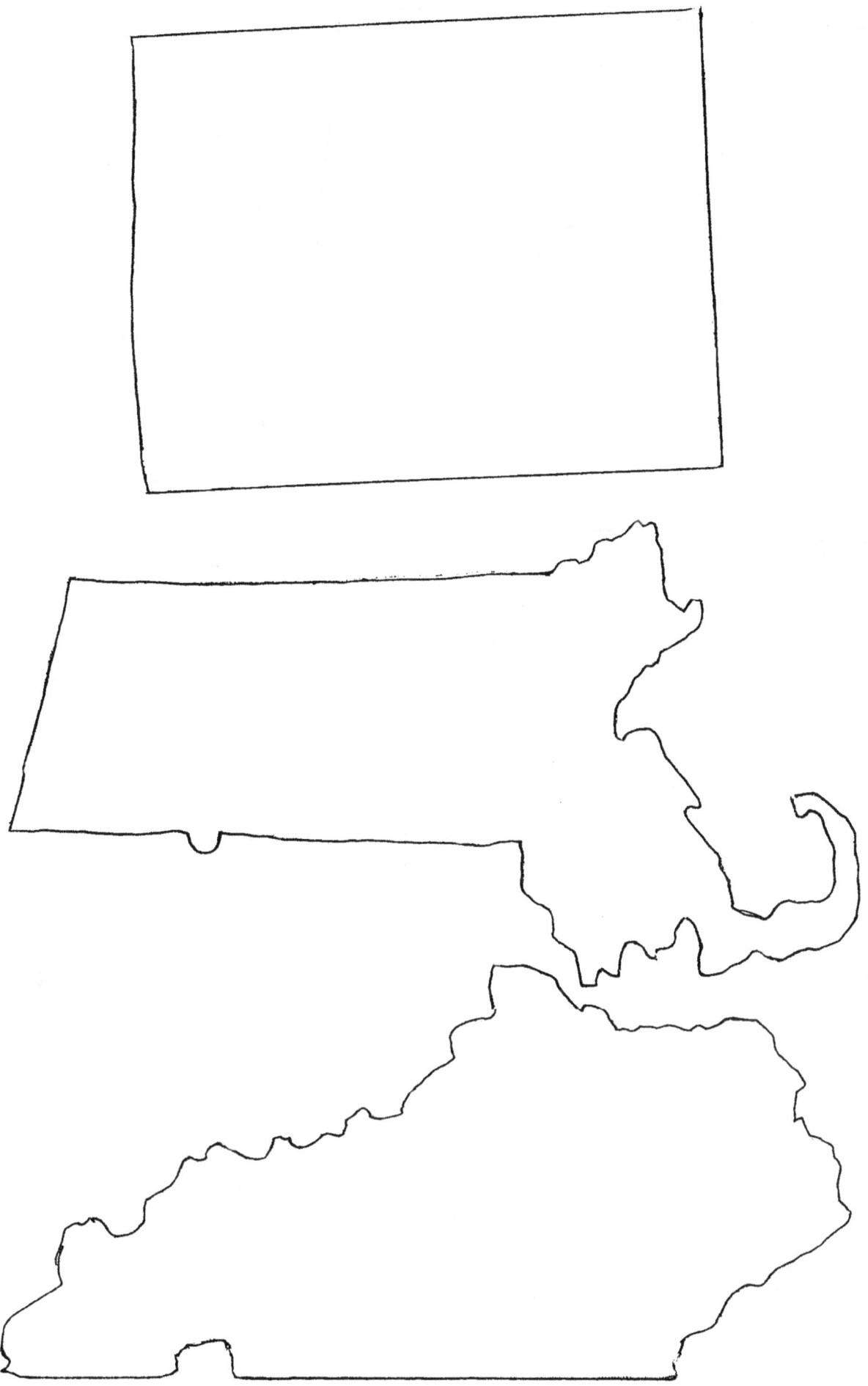

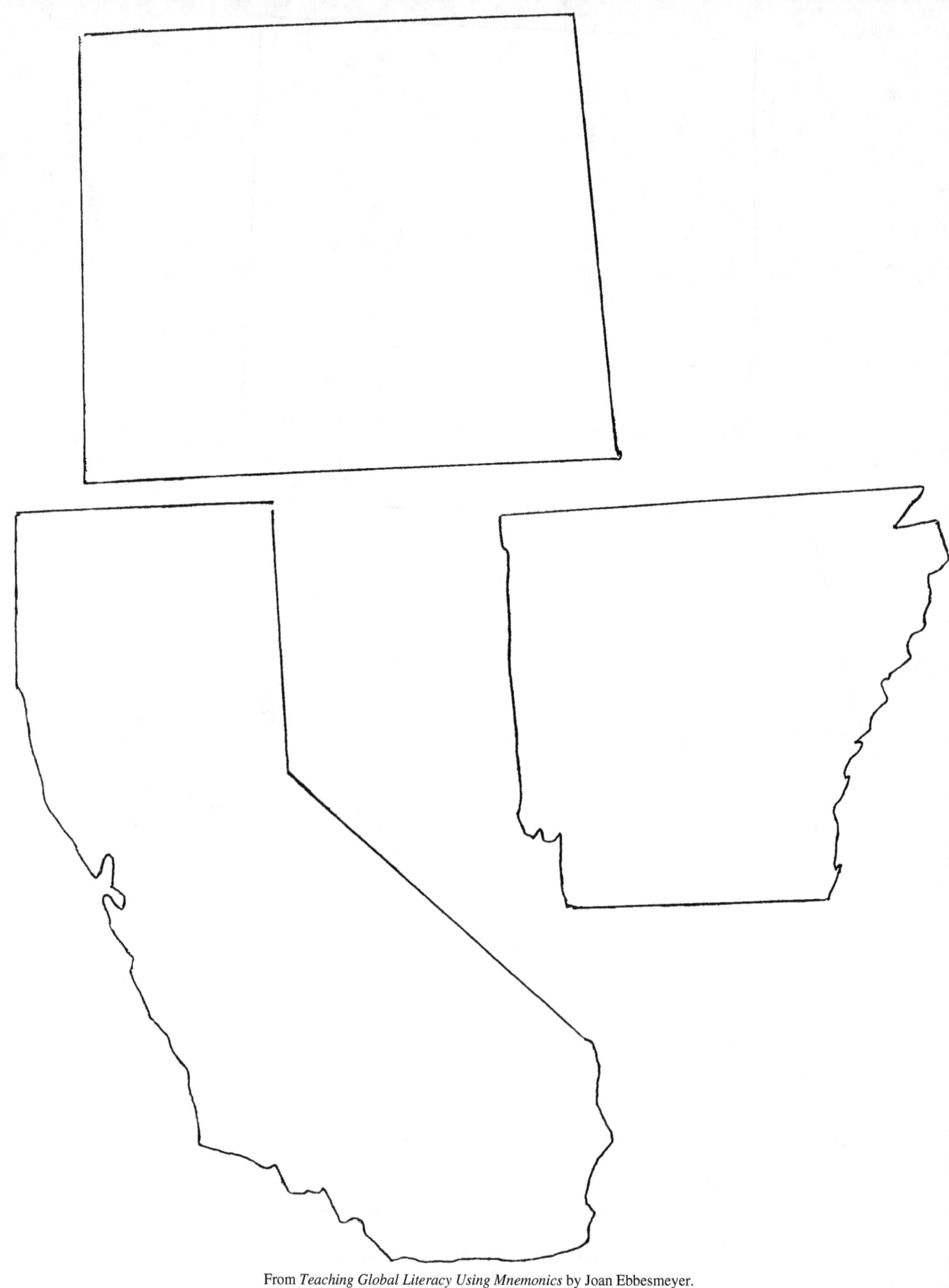

From *Teaching Global Literacy Using Mnemonics* by Joan Ebbesmeyer.
Westport, CT: Libraries Unlimited/Teacher Ideas Press. Copyright © 2006.

From *Teaching Global Literacy Using Mnemonics* by Joan Ebbesmeyer.
Westport, CT: Libraries Unlimited/Teacher Ideas Press. Copyright © 2006.

From *Teaching Global Literacy Using Mnemonics* by Joan Ebbesmeyer.
Westport, CT: Libraries Unlimited/Teacher Ideas Press. Copyright © 2006.

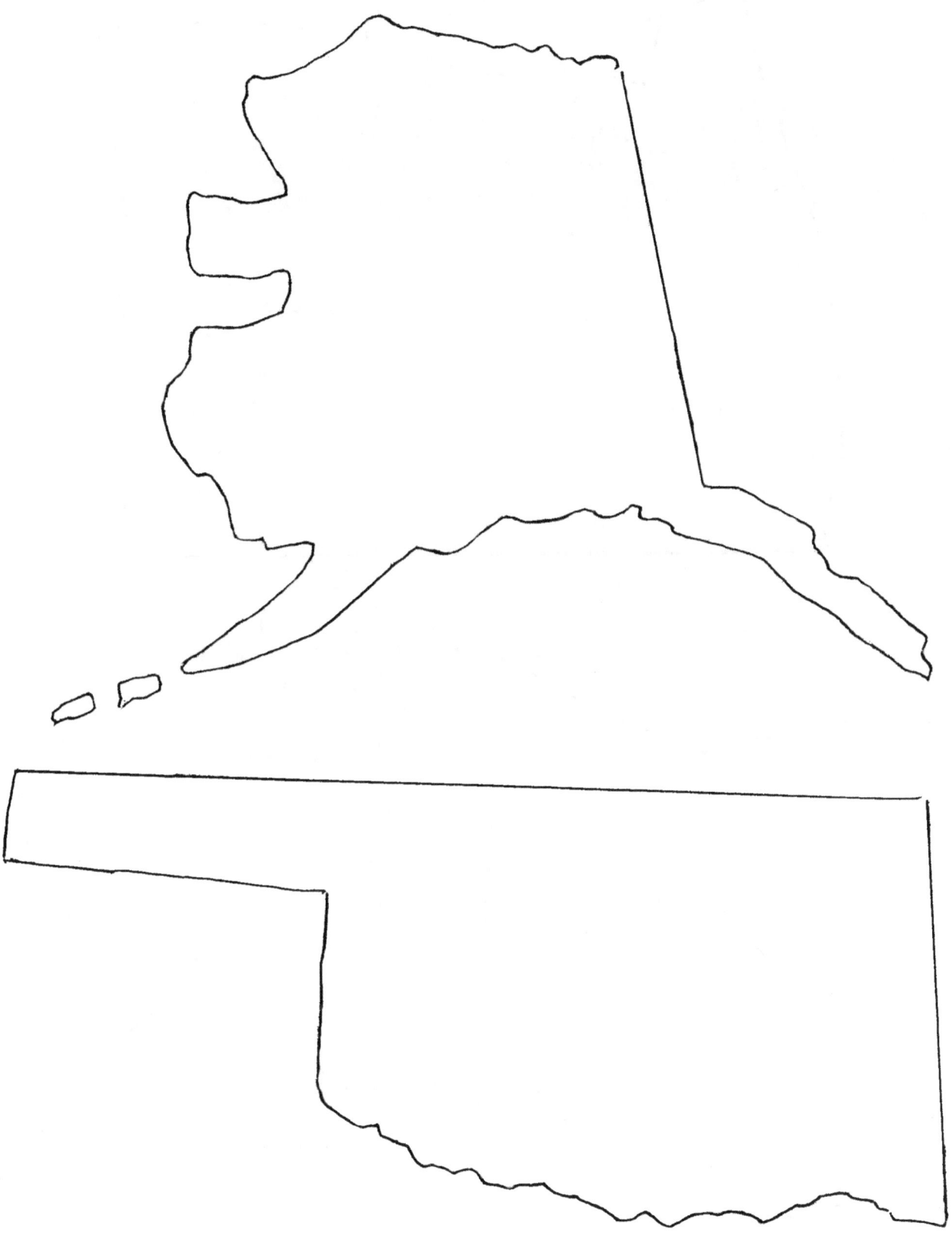

From *Teaching Global Literacy Using Mnemonics* by Joan Ebbesmeyer.
Westport, CT: Libraries Unlimited/Teacher Ideas Press. Copyright © 2006.

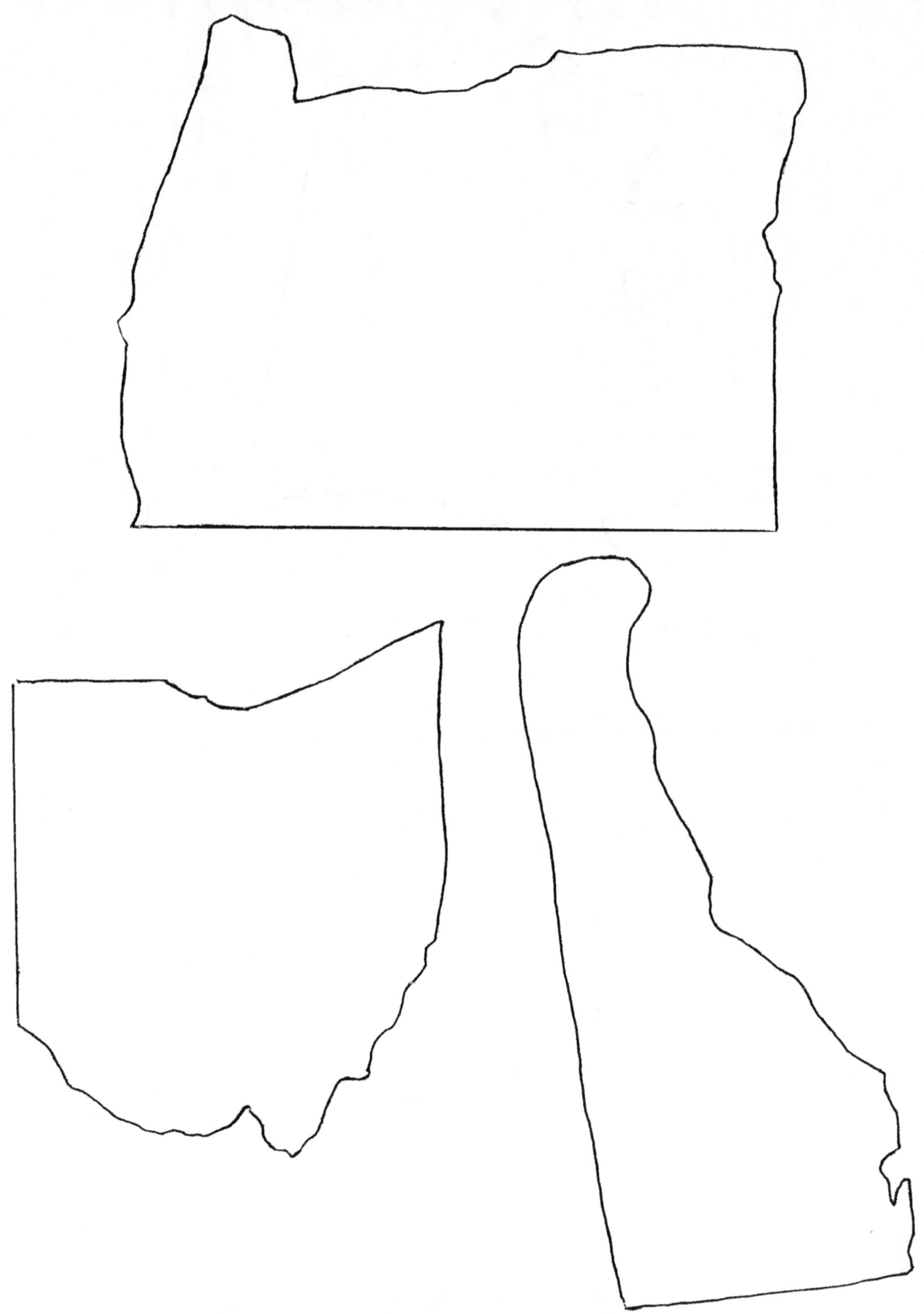

From *Teaching Global Literacy Using Mnemonics* by Joan Ebbesmeyer.
Westport, CT: Libraries Unlimited/Teacher Ideas Press. Copyright © 2006.

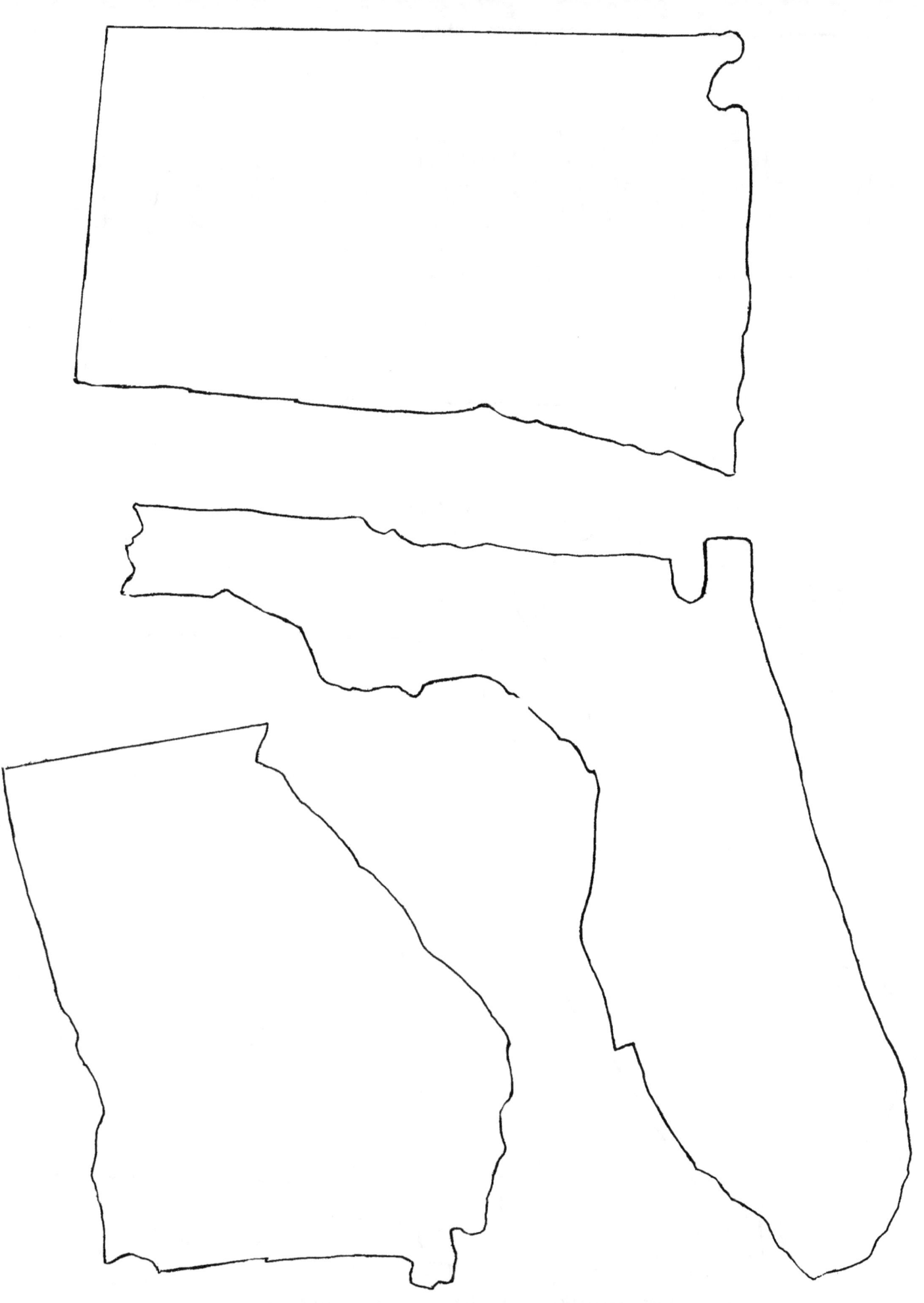

From *Teaching Global Literacy Using Mnemonics* by Joan Ebbesmeyer.
Westport, CT: Libraries Unlimited/Teacher Ideas Press. Copyright © 2006.

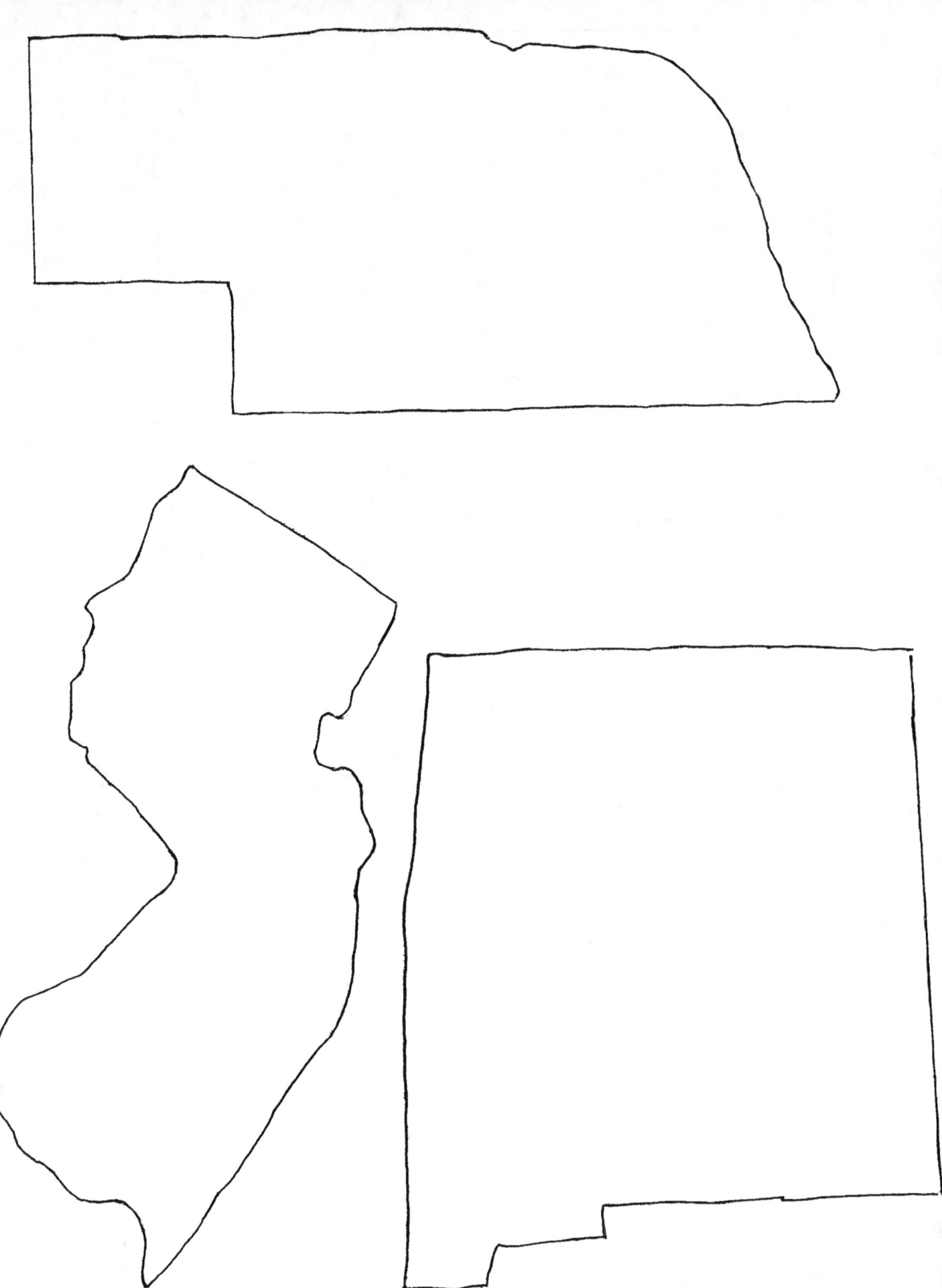

From *Teaching Global Literacy Using Mnemonics* by Joan Ebbesmeyer.
Westport, CT: Libraries Unlimited/Teacher Ideas Press. Copyright © 2006.

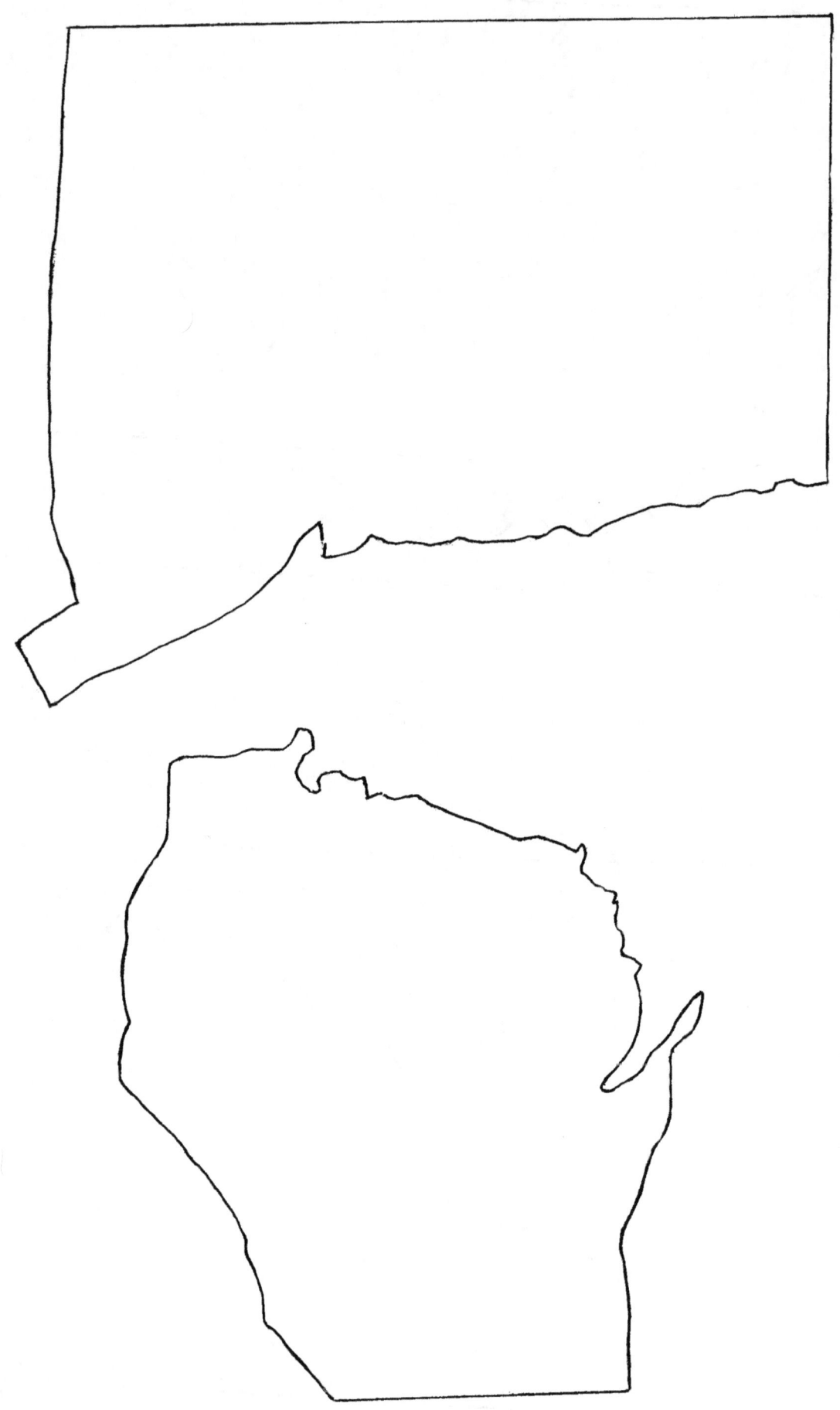

From *Teaching Global Literacy Using Mnemonics* by Joan Ebbesmeyer.
Westport, CT: Libraries Unlimited/Teacher Ideas Press. Copyright © 2006.

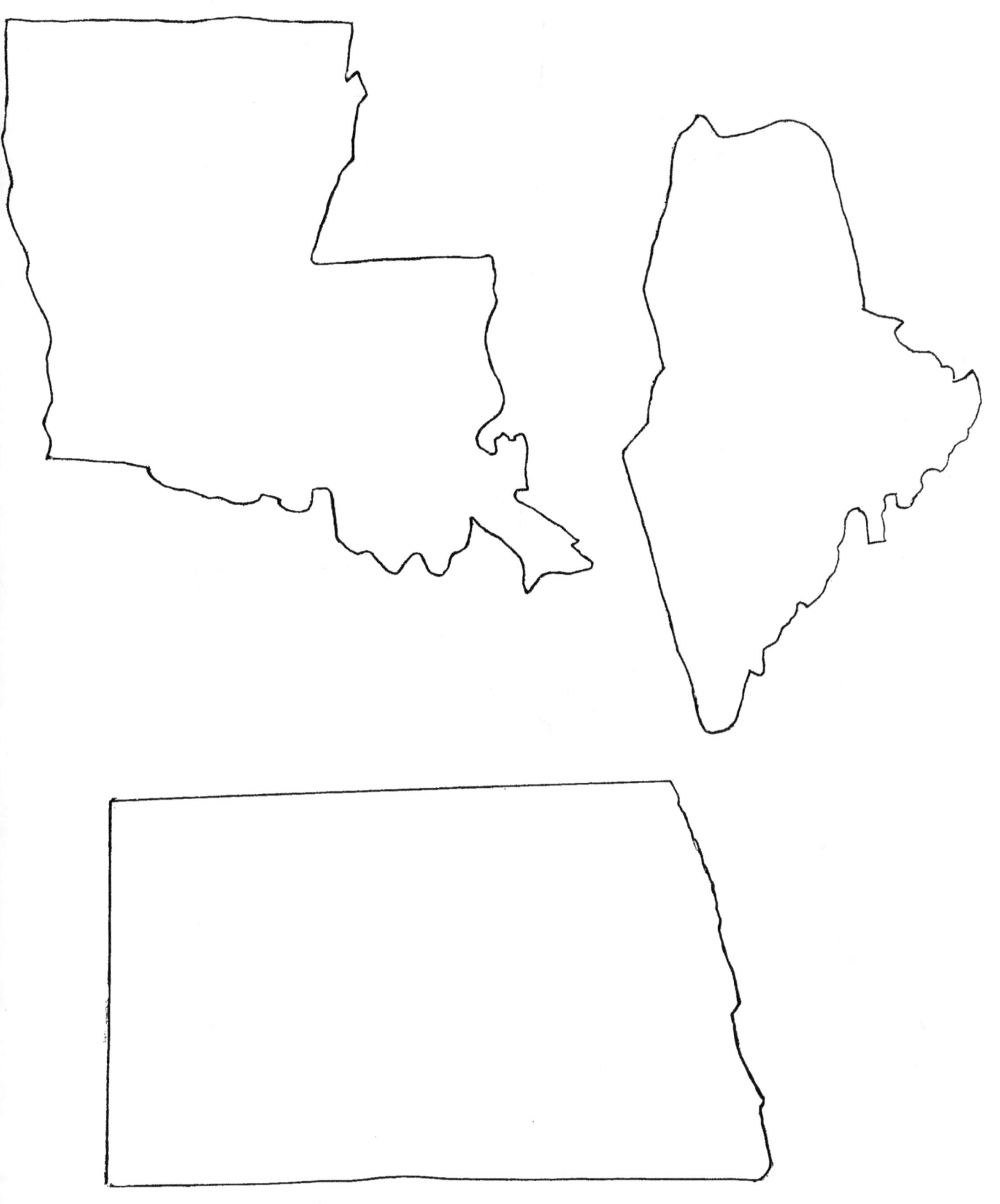

From *Teaching Global Literacy Using Mnemonics* by Joan Ebbesmeyer.
Westport, CT: Libraries Unlimited/Teacher Ideas Press. Copyright © 2006.

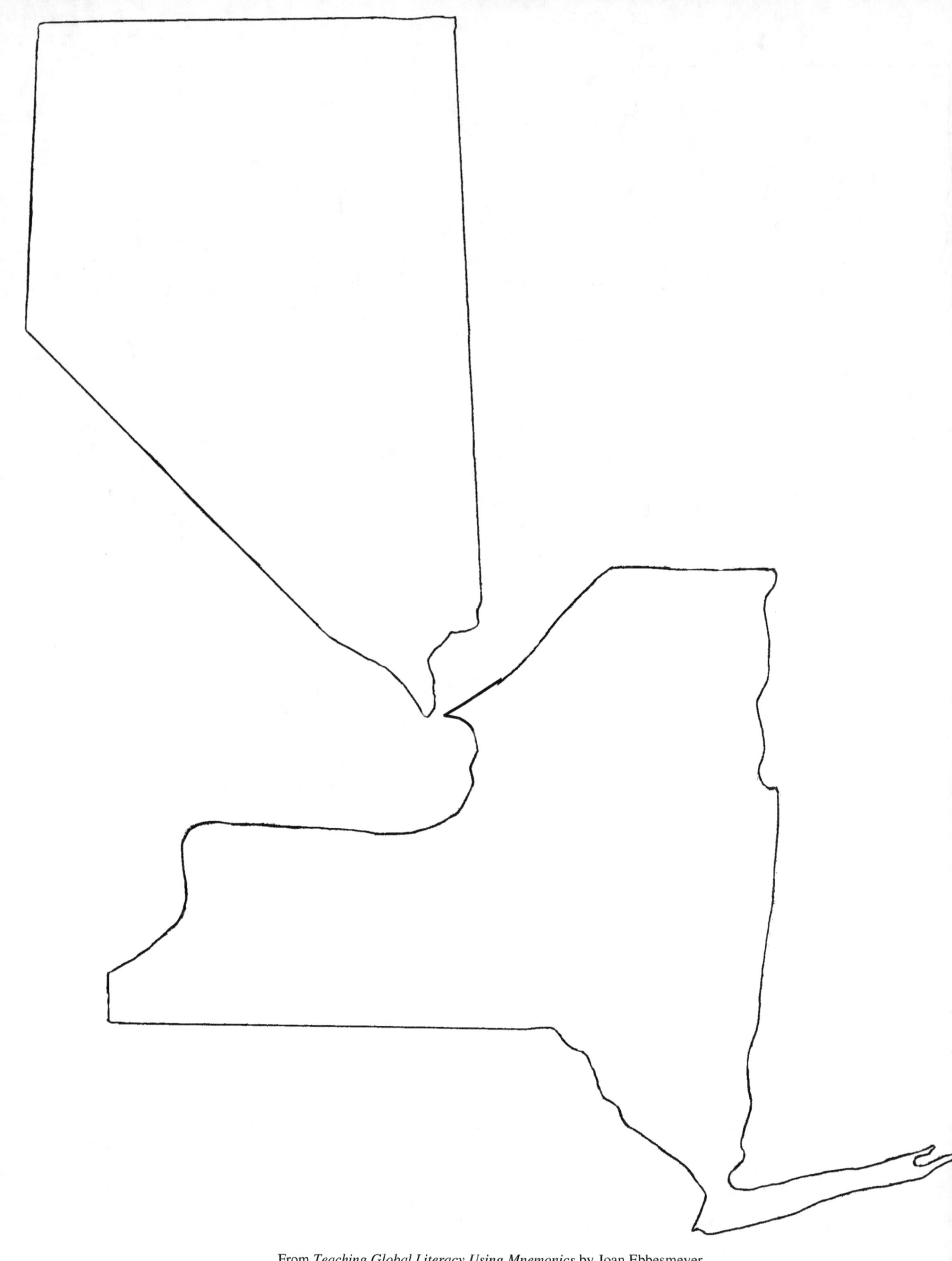

From *Teaching Global Literacy Using Mnemonics* by Joan Ebbesmeyer.
Westport, CT: Libraries Unlimited/Teacher Ideas Press. Copyright © 2006.

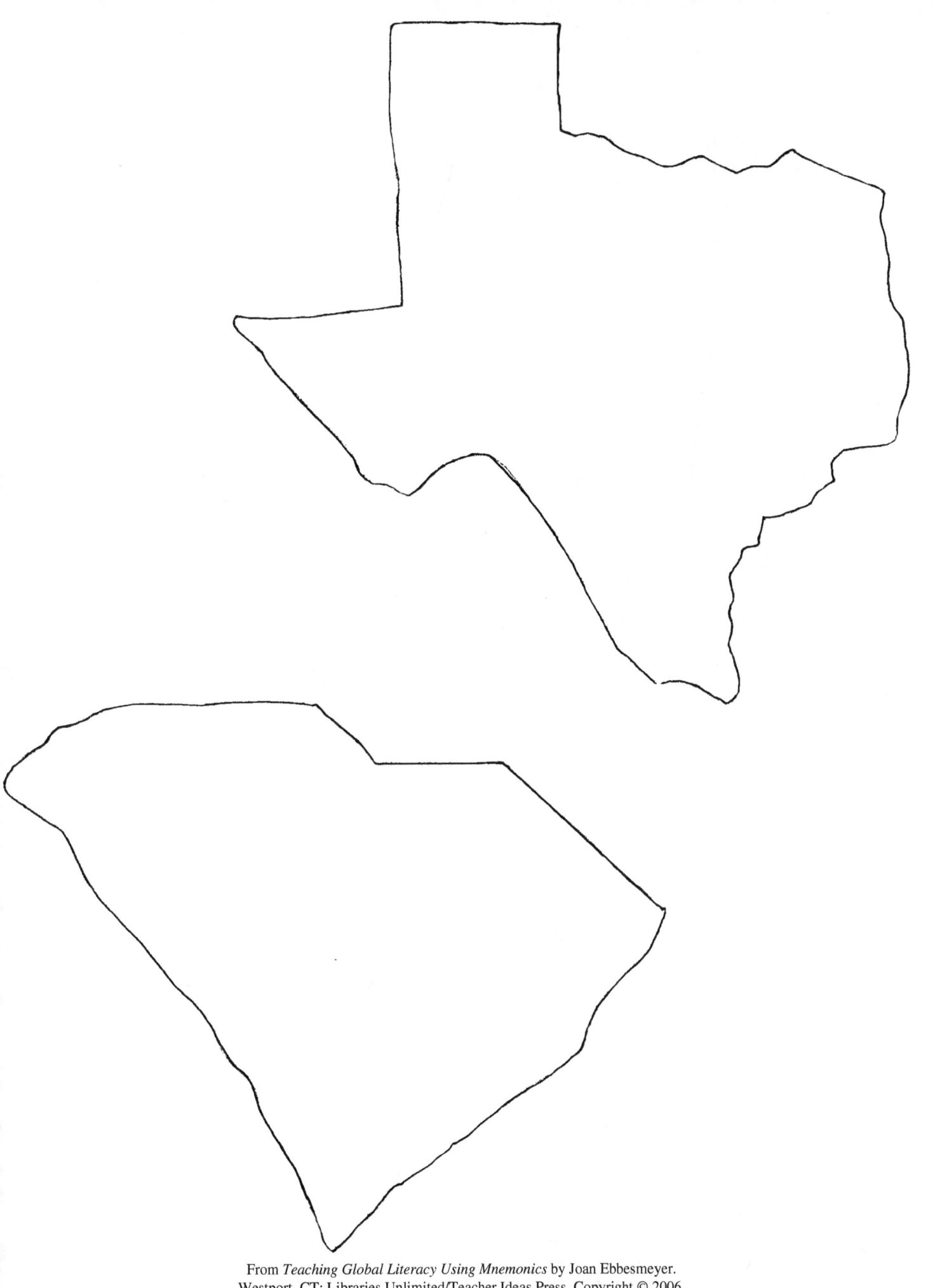

From *Teaching Global Literacy Using Mnemonics* by Joan Ebbesmeyer.
Westport, CT: Libraries Unlimited/Teacher Ideas Press. Copyright © 2006.

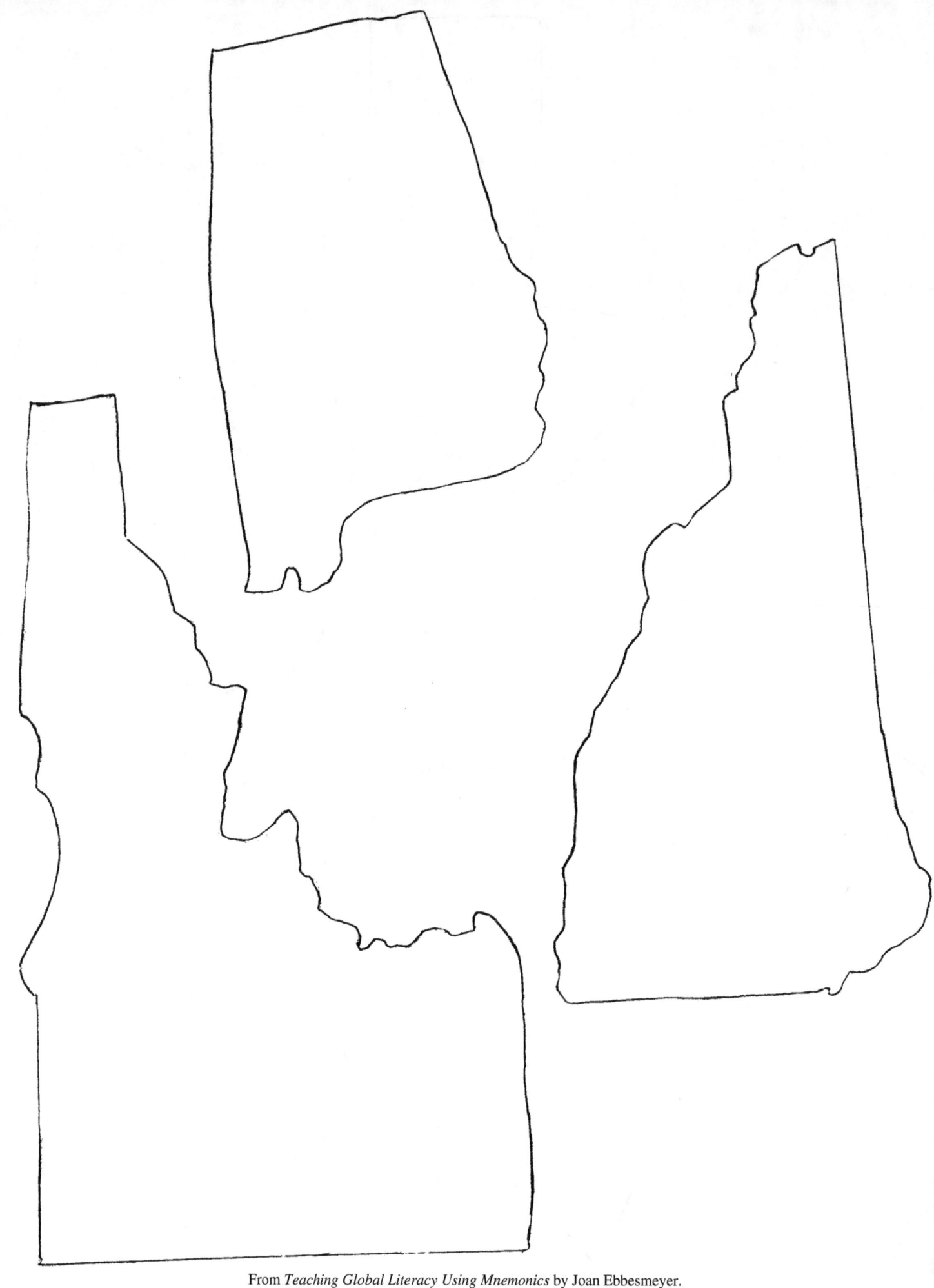

United States Activities: Connections, Association, and Webbing (Standards 7, 9, 12, 14, and 17)

New England States

Clue Questions

A short recounting of the life of a famous person could help students remember the six New England states. Use these ten questions and the life story of Emily Dickinson as an introduction to the fifty-state study. Allow any answers or guesses students might offer as you discuss these questions to pique their interest.

Ten Questions to Reveal the Identity of Emily Dickinson

1. Who was the mysterious woman in white from New England who wandered around her home late at night and wrote beautiful poetry?
2. Why did she write almost two thousand poems yet make little effort to have them published?
3. Why did she never marry the men she loved so deeply?
4. Why did she become a recluse in her mid-twenties?
5. She called her house, "My Father's house." In which of the New England States was the house located?
6. Why did she always dress in white?
7. Why didn't she go to church, even though her father and grandfather were church leaders in the town?
8. Considering that she saw only her yard and garden from her window, not the town or other people, what do you think was the theme of many of her poems?
9. After her death, who finally found her hundreds of poems and had them published?
10. Her first name was Emily. What was her last name?

After all answers and guesses have been made, hand out an information sheet that correctly answers all of these questions. Include one of Emily Dickinson's wonderful poems.

Information Sheet: Emily Dickinson

The mysterious woman in white was the famous poet, Emily Dickinson. She wrote many poems but did not think them worthy of publication.

Emily lived during the 1800s in the town of Amherst, Massachusetts. She was a pretty and very intelligent girl, who was allowed to further her education. This was a rather rare thing for young ladies in that day and age. However, the school was rigid and offered little social life for a young, pretty girl yearning for life and romance.

Emily returned home to her "father's house" and slowly became a recluse; rarely leaving the house and the upstairs rooms where she roamed at night.

No one knows for sure why she chose the reclusive life. She never married, although she loved several men. Perhaps that is why she dressed, at all times, in virginal white.

Emily's father and grandfather were church leaders in the town of Amherst, Massachusetts, but Emily found God in nature and her garden rather than in church. The flowers, trees, and animals of her garden were the theme of many of her poems. They were her world!

After Emily died, her sister found more than fifteen hundred of her poems. She sent them to a friend in the publishing business, and Emily Dickinson became immortalized in the beautiful verses that are today read around the world.

Here is the beginning of one of Dickinson's poems:

> Frequently the woods are pink —
> Frequently are brown.
> Frequently the hills undress
> Behind my native town.

She wrote about how *frequently* trees are pink,

But at other times, they *frequently* were brown (repetition in lines 1 and 2)

She described them as *undressing, at times,* (personification in line 3)

(Behind her little town)

Once students have learned about Emily Dickinson and the New England States, especially the most northern *cold* state, Maine, they can associate the region with a mnemonic sentence to remember them as the first six states of northeast America.

Maine **N**eeds **V**ery **M**any **C**old **R**eliefs.

1. **M**aine
2. **N**ew Hampshire
3. **V**ermont
4. **M**assachusetts
5. **C**onnecticut
6. **R**hode Island

After filling in the first six states of their maps and learning about the beauty of nature found in the New England region, students may be encouraged to write poems patterned on Emily Dickinson's one about trees, a portion of which appears on the Information Sheet. She used the word repetition of "frequently" in the first three lines, and personification is used in the third line. There are many things in nature (sun, river, clouds, stars, rain) to pattern from this poem.

Example:

Frequently the stars shine bright,
Frequently they glow.
Frequently they guard the sky,
While on their night patrol.

—Composed by a fourth-grade student

Midwestern States

The "Show-Me State"

Identify the only state that has a shape with a "boot heel": Missouri. This state is in the heartland, and explain that the term is used because the region is in the approximate middle of the continent, but a little to the right (just like the location of the human heart).

Discuss the historical state of Missouri, where the Pony Express started and the famous Oregon and Santa Fe Trails began. Lewis and Clark embarked on their famous expedition from this area, and today we find the great St. Louis Arch there, which commemorates the Western Expansion. Missouri is truly the "Gateway to the West."

Missouri borders eight states. What are their names?

Missouri is shown in the middle of the nine-state map below. The capital cities of the eight states bordering it are as follows:

1. Des Moines   2. Springfield   3. Frankfort   4. Nashville
5. Little Rock   6. Lincoln   7. Topeka   8. Oklahoma City

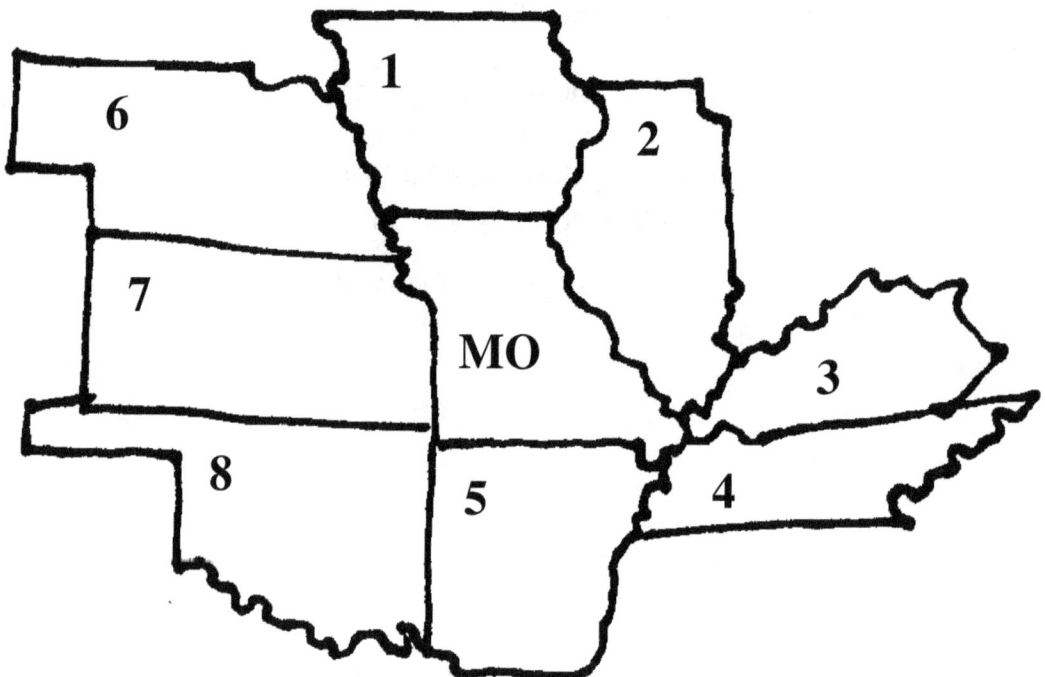

Western States: The West Is Best!

Read the book *Prairie* by Diane Siebert
    Trace the Oregon and Santa Fe Trails and the western trip of Lewis and Clark, along the Missouri River, to learn most of the western states. Identify the states as you make your imaginary trip west. Allow groups to choose the trip they like best. Students could write stories of experiences they have along the way.

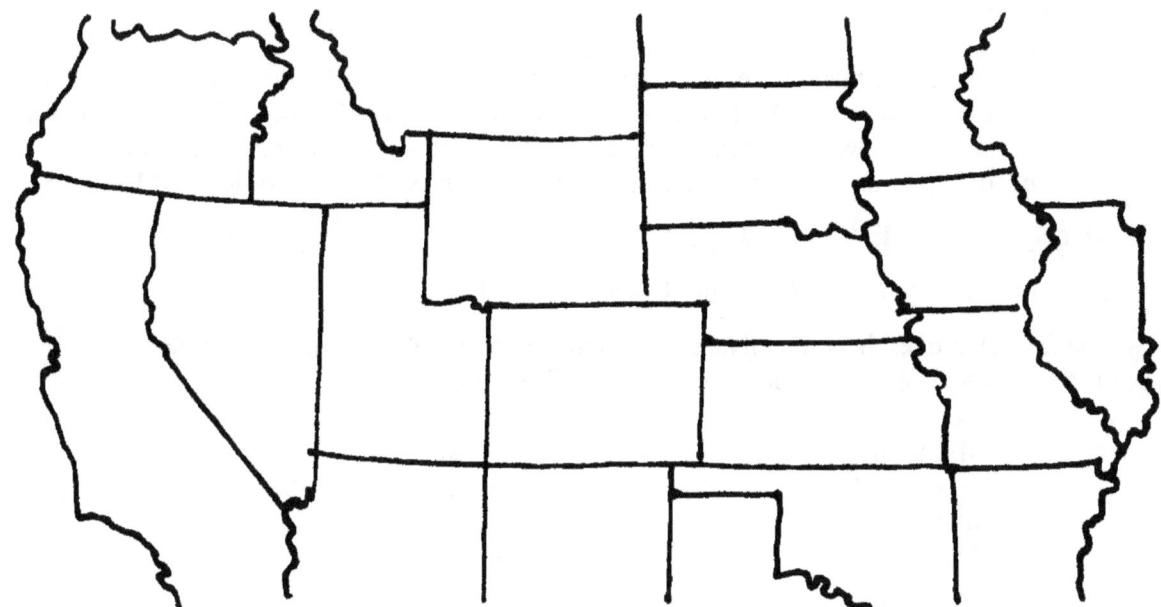

The Mighty Mississippi

The Mississippi River and Bordering States

Read the book *Mississippi* by Diane Siebert
   The mighty Mississippi River is a fascinating thing to study. Brave pioneers like DeSoto, La Salle, and Marquette discovered it. Tall Tales such as the escapades of Mike Fink tell about the river, as do books such as *Huckleberry Finn* by Mark Twain, and there are exciting river cities and states along the Mississippi's banks. All these can serve to motivate students to study the region further.

Students can see the many waterways (tributaries) that flow into the great river, which divides the country from north to south. As it flows south past Illinois, it is fed from the big Illinois River as well as many others. The waters are rushing south to the Mississippi lowlands and to the sea!
   With this information, you can create a mnemonic for the states that border the Mississippi:

Many **W**aterways **I**n **I**llinois **M**erge,

Knowing **T**hey **A**mplify **M**ississippi **L**owlands.

The first letter of each word will help them remember the states that are located along the Mississippi River, in succession, from north to south. (Define "amplify.")

Minnesota	**K**entucky
Wisconsin	**T**ennessee
Iowa	**A**rkansas
Illinois	**M**ississippi
Missouri	**L**ouisiana

Trace the Mississippi on the large class map, and have students do the same on their individual maps. Then fill in the state names from left to right, starting with Minnesota and ending with Louisiana.

United States Activities: Poetry Connections

All States and Land Formations

   Diane Siebert's geographical poetry draws us to an appreciation of the land and a desire to know more about the wonders of this great country of ours. The illustrations of Wendell Minor in combination with her creative rhymes can lure students to learn of the regions about which she writes.
   Sierra is her powerful and compelling book about the mountains.
   Animals, weather, plants, and land formations are all part of the information found in this book. The four types of land formations considered mountains can be associated with the mnemonic of *shapes*. One is shaped round at the top like a **dome**. The second is shaped in a square like a **block**. The third is shaped like a hand fan, **fold**ed on itself. The fourth type of mountain has a crater at its top and is called a **volcano**.

   1. **Dome** (round) mountains

   2. **Block** (square) mountains

3. **Fold** (fan) mountains

4. **Volcano** (crater) mountains

The Rocky and Appalachian mountain states can be identified on the western and eastern sides of the map, after reading *Sierra*. Allow students to draw mountains across these states. Have them research and draw dome, block, fold, and volcano mountains.

Mojave is Siebert's book on deserts. It is exciting and beautifully illustrated. It can be used as a way to interest students in learning about the five U.S. deserts, which stretch across ten states.

One of the deserts, the Sonoran Desert, contains the wondrous giant cactus plant called the saguaro (sag-WAR-o). This plant takes more than one hundred years to reach full maturity and can live for two hundred years. It can protect man and beast, insect and serpent from the perils of the desert. Even in death, the saguaro continues to provide.

Giant of the Desert

Look in the library for a picture book on the saguaro cactus. Learning about this interesting plant leads to a mnemonic on the American deserts.

Saguaro **C**actuses **M**ake **N**oble **G**iants.

Sonoran

Chihuahua

Mojave

Navajo

Great Basin

Label the ten desert states on the map below.
Clue: The four states at the bottom all border Mexico!

From *Teaching Global Literacy Using Mnemonics* by Joan Ebbesmeyer.
Westport, CT: Libraries Unlimited/Teacher Ideas Press. Copyright © 2006.

Heartland and Mississippi

After hearing the moving words of Siebert's *Heartland,* encourage a discussion about why some states are located in what is called the "Heartland of America." Allow students to fill in any Midwest states they can identify or write a pattern poem about them.

> I am the Heartland; hear my beat
> I am where great rivers meet
> With summer, winter, but none too long.
> I sing my country's wondrous song.

1. As you read one page at a time of Siebert's *Mississippi,* allow students to draw about what they hear. Give them some time. Then show the illustrations by Greg Harlin to compare and contrast their feelings with his about the great river.

2. Create a bulletin board of their drawings.

3. Allow the use of the first line of the poem to write a pattern poem about any world river.

> I am the river; ancient now,
> But once I made the pharaohs bow.
> When every year, I caused the flood,
> And spilled the Nile's life-giving mud.

"I Hear America Singing"

Walt Whitman wrote his unrhymed poem to celebrate the workers of America. The carpenters, masons, shoemakers, boatmen and others, were all honored in this classic hymn.

After learning of the many varied areas and land regions of the United States, students could be encouraged to hear the other sounds of this vast land. They could be encouraged to make a list and write about the many sounds and sights, and the feelings inspired by its cities, peoples, rural areas, rivers, farms, or oceans. This could be turned into a rhymed or unrhymed poem about America.

Example:

Sounds of America

I hear the sounds of America,
The sounds that make us boast,
Of that great land that stretches out,
From the eastern to western coast.

The sounds come from the oceans,
And frame the mighty land.
Their waves send up a chorus,
That crashes, loud and grand.

The sounds come from the mountains,
From snow-capped, jagged peaks,
They call out to the valley,
And the sky it seems to tries to seek.

—*Written as a pattern poem by a sixth-grade student*

United States Activities: States' History and Geography

Quarter Quandary (Standards 7, 9, 12, 14, and 17)

The United States Mint began a program in 1999 to honor each of the fifty states with a new commemorative quarter.

Motivate interest by allowing students to make a quarter map of the ones they collect and tape to the correct unlabeled state map. Parents might want to be a part of this project.

The "money maps" should be kept in a special place. Students might want to choose an environmental or charitable organization to contribute the quarters when the project is completed.

United States Activities: Math

Commemorative Quarters

We have fifty states in the United States. The U.S. Mint will commemorate the same number of states each year for ten years. How many states does it honor each year? _____

The first new quarters were minted in 1999. What year is (or was) the last year for quarters to be minted? _____

How many new quarters were minted by 2005? _____

How many more will need to be minted to finish the fifty quarters? _____

Vocabulary: Quarters

The U.S. Mint will send you a small pamphlet about their quarter program, if you write to

Department of the Treasury

United States Mint

Washington, DC 20220

In that pamphlet, there are words you need to understand. See if you can define the following underlined words by how they are used in the paragraph.

The U.S. Mint will <u>commemorate</u> each U.S. state. It wants young people to celebrate our nation and create a treasured <u>legacy</u>. It is a way to honor our country's <u>heritage</u>. The coins <u>depict</u> the history, geography, and <u>diversity</u> of our nation. The coins are legal <u>tender</u>. There are two sides to the coin. George Washington will continue to be shown on the <u>obverse</u> side, and the reverse side will have a special design for each state.

From *Teaching Global Literacy Using Mnemonics* by Joan Ebbesmeyer.
Westport, CT: Libraries Unlimited/Teacher Ideas Press. Copyright © 2006.

Research: Quarters

Researching the commemorative quarters can produce endless opportunities for learning! Students can discover why the Great Lakes are depicted on the Michigan quarter and why there is a large star pictured on that for Texas. The Florida quarter can lead to a study on space travel or the exciting stories of the sixteenth-century Spanish galleons, whose sunken treasures are now being discovered and retrieved. Each student could choose a state coin and create a page to explain the depictions. The students turn the pages into a book and give it as a gift to the school library.

U.S. Activities: Creative Thinking (Standards 1, 13–16)

Fluency

Some students will know the location of their own state or states they have visited. Provide an individual map for students and allow them to label all the state locations they know. If they work in pairs, there may be disagreements about locations. This should be allowed and used as a learning tool as the project goes on.

Flexibility

Make sure all the students have identified the location of their own state. Allow them to list the things that make their state important, beautiful, or unique, then have them think of their state as an animal, person, or thing. This is "personification."

Missouri could be a donkey because its motto, the "Show Me State" implies that it's stubborn.

Florida could be a snake because of its shape.

Washington is a president, **Delaware** is a number 1, **Michigan** is a mitten, **Massachusetts** is a shoe, **Arizona** is a canyon, and so on.

Researching state facts on the Internet or in an encyclopedia will give students ideas and information and allow them to think in flexible ways.

Originality

After learning about your state (or about another of your choosing), see how many alliterative sentences you can write about it. (Have students use a thesaurus.)
Example:
Arizona is almost always hot, but air-conditioning aids, and the state's attractions are awesome!
(Be prepared to name some of the awesome attractions!)

Elaboration

Add on to the state project by creating a fifty-page "Most Important" book, with a page for each state. Include a map of the state and a paragraph or two on its importance.
(See example for Arizona that follows.)

Arizona

A map of the state of Arizona.

Arizona is important because it is the home of one of America's great deserts, the Sonoran; it's the only place you'll find the giant Saguaro cactus!

Arizona is important because irrigation and the Glen Canyon Dam have transformed desert land into rich farmland.

Arizona is important for its large Indian reservations, its Painted Desert, its Petrified Forest, and its great monuments.

BUT

The most important thing about Arizona is:

It is the home of the GRAND CANYON!

Make a similar page for the rest of the forty-nine states.

Create a book!

From *Teaching Global Literacy Using Mnemonics* by Joan Ebbesmeyer.
Westport, CT: Libraries Unlimited/Teacher Ideas Press. Copyright © 2006.

U.S. State Map Clues

1. This state is named after the first President of the United States.

   It borders Canada and the Pacific Ocean.

2. Salt Lake City is the capital city of this state.

   It lies between Nevada and Colorado.

3. This state is shaped like a glove.

   This state is almost completely surrounded by the Great Lakes.

4. This state was named after Queen Mary of England.

   Washington D.C. is very close to it.

5. This state has two words in its name. The first is "West."

   It is directly west of Virginia.

6. This is one of the "North" and "South" states (that is, the word "North" or "South" is in its name.

   It borders Canada on the north.

7. This is one of the eight states that border Missouri.

   It is directly north of Missouri.

8. This is one of the second "North" and "South" states.

   It is north of South Carolina.

9. The "Aloha State" is made up of volcanic islands.

   It is found in the Pacific Ocean.

10. This state has the major city of Chicago.

    It's another state that borders Missouri, sitting to its east.

11. This state was named after the longest river in the United States.

    It is between Alabama and Louisiana.

*From Teaching Global Literacy Using Mnemonics by Joan Ebbesmeyer.
Westport, CT: Libraries Unlimited/Teacher Ideas Press. Copyright © 2006.*

12. Minneapolis is the capital of this northern state.

    It touches Canada on the north and Iowa on the south.

13. This state has many mountains, and you'll find the capital city of Denver there.

    Shaped like a block, it lies below another block-shaped state, Wyoming.

14. This state is shaped like an elf's shoe, and Boston is the capital.

    The shoe is stepping on Connecticut and Rhode Island.

15. This is the state that Daniel Boone left to travel to Missouri.

    Just a small section of the state borders Missouri on the east.

16. This is the last to be listed in the alphabetical order of the fifty states.

    Part of this state is directly beneath Montana.

17. You'll find San Francisco and Los Angeles in this state.

    If you go any farther west, you'll end up in the Pacific Ocean.

18. It's called the Land of Opportunity, and Little Rock is the capital.

    The whole state borders Missouri on the north.

19. Find the Wabash River running through this state.

    It's just east of another "I" state, Illinois.

20. The "Show Me State" has St. Louis and the Arch.

    It's in the heart of the country, and it has eight states bordering it.

21. This state was named after William Penn.

    You will find it south of the state of New York.

22. This is the smallest state in the United States.

    It's next to Connecticut.

23. It's shape is similar to a "V," and the name starts with a V.

    It's located between two "News"—New York and New Hampshire.

24. We find the Grand Canyon here, and Phoenix is the capital.

    You'll find California to the west and Mexico to the south.

*From Teaching Global Literacy Using Mnemonics by Joan Ebbesmeyer.
Westport, CT: Libraries Unlimited/Teacher Ideas Press. Copyright © 2006.*

25. This state is cold and not connected to the original forty-eight states.
    It borders Canada on the west.

26. They say this state is OK! The state and its song have the same name.
    It's west of Arkansas and touches a small part of Missouri.

27. This state was the end of a famous trail, traveled by pioneers in the 1800s.
    The state is situated between Washington and California. It touches the Pacific.

28. This state has three big "C" cities: Cincinnati, Cleveland, and Columbus.
    This state is right beneath Michigan and Lake Erie.

29. It's shaped something like an L and was the first state to join the union.
    This small state is squeezed between Maryland and New Jersey.

30. This state is the southern part of the Dakotas.
    It is directly south of North Dakota.

31. This is a southern state. It's one of the peninsula states and looks like a finger.
    This state is under Alabama and Georgia, and it has oceans on three sides.

32. Atlanta is the capital of this state.
    This state is just above Florida.

33. It's another of the eight states touching Missouri. It's called the cornhusker state.
    South Dakota is on the north, and Kansas is on the south of this state.

34. It's one of the "New" states, and the second word in its name starts with a J.
    This small state is squeezed between Pennsylvania and the Atlantic Ocean.

35. Another "New" state that's named after the country to the south of it.
    This southwestern state lies between Arizona and Texas.

36. It's the fourth largest state, but not many people live there.
    It borders Canada, Idaho, and the Dakotas.

37. "The Tennessee Waltz" is the state song, and Nashville is the capital.
    The state is south of Kentucky and touches a small part of Missouri.

38. The first English settlement was here. Eight U.S. presidents were born here.

    It looks like a small mountain between West Virginia and the Atlantic Ocean.

39. This small state was the fifth to join the union. The capital is Hartford.

    It's connected to Rhode Island, sitting under Massachusetts.

40. Everyone thinks about cheese when they think of this state.

    "On Wisconsin" is its state song!

41. You'll find New Orleans in this state.

    This state lies where the mighty Mississippi River empties into the Gulf of Mexico.

42. Did they name it because they thought it was a "main" state?

    It's high in the north, located between Canada, New Hampshire, and the Atlantic.

43. One of the "North" states, the climate here is cold, and Bismarck is the capital.

    This state is directly north of South Dakota.

44. Many people travel to this state to gamble in the casinos of Las Vegas.

    From this state, you travel west to California or east to Utah.

45. It's the "Big Apple" state. You can see the Statue of Liberty here.

    This large state is between Canada and Pennsylvania.

46. The "Lone Star State" is the second largest in the United States.

    If you travel south, you'll reach Mexico or the Gulf of Mexico.

47. Same name, only "South" of North Carolina.

    This is the smallest state in the South.

48. This is the southern state between Mississippi and Georgia.

    The first capital of the Confederacy was in this state.

49. It looks like this state has a chimney top.

    It borders all of Washington and Oregon on the west.

50. The last "New" state is one of the original thirteen.

    You'll find it tucked between Vermont and Maine.

From *Teaching Global Literacy Using Mnemonics* by Joan Ebbesmeyer.
Westport, CT: Libraries Unlimited/Teacher Ideas Press. Copyright © 2006.

Location, Location, Location!

Check your map to see if you have labeled all the states correctly according to the clues.

1. Washington
2. Utah
3. Michigan
4. Maryland
5. West Virginia
6. North Dakota
7. Iowa
8. North Carolina
9. Hawaii
10. Illinois
11. Mississippi
12. Minnesota
13. Colorado
14. Massachusetts
15. Kentucky
16. Wyoming
17. California
18. Arkansas
19. Indiana
20. Missouri
21. Pennsylvania
22. Rhode Island
23. Vermont
24. Arizona
25. Alaska
26. Oklahoma
27. Oregon
28. Ohio
29. Delaware
30. South Dakota
31. Florida
32. Georgia
33. Nebraska
34. New Jersey
35. New Mexico
36. Montana
37. Tennessee
38. Virginia
39. Connecticut
40. Wisconsin
41. Louisiana
42. Maine
43. North Dakota
44. Nevada
45. New York
46. Texas
47. South Carolina
48. Alabama
49. Idaho
50. New Hampshire

From Teaching Global Literacy Using Mnemonics by Joan Ebbesmeyer. Westport, CT: Libraries Unlimited/Teacher Ideas Press. Copyright © 2006.

Chapter 2

Central America and Mexico

Central America

Map of Mexico (Our Southern Neighbor)

Central America and Mexico

Central America connects North America to South America. Mexico, part of North America, is larger than all seven of the small countries that lie to the south of it in Central America. But Mexico has much in common with the small countries of Central America. The climate is hot and steamy in Mexico and in Central America. Furthermore, the native peoples of these regions suffered under Spanish rule for centuries. The Spanish left their language, their Catholic religion, and many descendants of Spanish and Indian origin, called *mestizos*.

Today Central American countries have all gained their political independence, but revolutions and unstable governments continue to cause suffering and poverty in many areas.

Suggested Reading

Books can excite interest in the geographic area while providing an opportunity to include world geography in the daily curriculum. Many excellent picture books are available to bring enjoyment and information to students of all ages. Chapter books are a favorite way to entice the older student to seek more information and conduct research to get it. The books suggested here are just that—suggestions. Many other books and stories could serve in their place.

Picture Books

Ada, Alma Flor. *The Gold Coin.* Illustrated by Neil Waldman. Maxwell Macmillan Int. Publishing Group, 1991.

    Juan is a thief who spies a gold coin in the house of Doña Josefa and decides to try to steal it from her. What he thinks will be a very easy robbery turns out to be a long journey through the Central American countryside, chasing the elusive woman who is determined to help anyone in need.

    Doña Josefa nurses and comforts all who ask for her help and also tries to give each of them her gold coin. Meanwhile, Juan's travels take him across rivers, over mountains, and through the valleys of Central America. He meets many people who help him in every way they can. They all tell him of the merciful actions of Doña Josefa.

    Juan does not succeed in gaining the golden treasure from the old lady. However, he finds a different and much more valuable treasure by the end of his journey.

Hess, Paul. *Rain Forest Animals.* Rhymes by Mel Gibson, Zarina Husain, Gail Kredenser, Jack Prelutsky, Carol Pike, John Travers Moore. De Agostini Editions, 1996.

    The animals found in the Central American rain forests are beautifully illustrated by Paul Hess and described in short, funny rhymes by several well-known authors. Most young children are familiar with monkeys, snakes, parrots, and jaguars, but the anteater, toucan, tapir, and tree frog might be interesting and novel animals for them to learn more about. They may find humor in the rhymes about tapirs picking up food with their noses and stomping with their stubby toes. And they will learn to be cautious around a sleeping snake because its jaws could still be awake! This book is a fun introduction for young students who are just beginning to learn about the rain forests.

Ryder, Joanne. *Jaguar in the Rain Forest.* Illustrated by Michael Rothman. Morrow Junior Books, 1996.

    This beautifully illustrated book takes the young reader on a lively, imaginative trip through the lush, green world of the rain forest. The reader becomes a jaguar as it climbs higher and higher into the vines and towering trees. You see the sights of the spider monkeys and soaring birds. You hear the sounds of buzzing, chattering, and howls of various animals.

Then you return to the jaguar's home on the floor of the jungle where the trees begin and the rivers flow. You can drink the cool water and swim to places where the hunting is good.

You add to the sounds with your great roar and wait until darkness to find your prey. Creeping silently through the thick underbrush, you leap with your powerful legs and catch the unsuspecting armadillo with your sharp claws. You have found your dinner for tonight.

You rest and feel the gentle raindrops on your back, bringing you back to reality while you dream of that place where monkeys howl and jaguars roar.

Yolen, Jane. *Welcome to the Green House.* Illustrated by Laura Regan. G. P. Putnam Sons, 1993.

The green house of the tropical jungle is presented to us as a kaleidoscope of color, with its blue hummingbirds, golden toads, silver fish, crimson flowers, and the multicolored snakes and butterflies housed in the endless shades of green—dark, light, emerald, and copper-green. There's a bright green, a blue green, and an ever-new green in this fascinating house.

Along with color, the house is described as a cacophony of sound created by the "a-hoo" of the howler monkey, the drone of the bees, the chitter-chatter of the birds, and the growl of the ocelot. The green house beckons us to open the door to the mysterious world of the rain forest!

Chapter Book

Alexander, Lloyd. *The Eldorado Adventure.* E. P. Dutton, 1987.

Can you imagine receiving a telegram informing you that you now own a volcano in the wild jungle of Central America? That's what happened to seventeen-year-old Vesper Holly!

Vesper can't wait to leave Philadelphia and sail away with her guardian, Professor Brinton Garrett. It seems like a great and exciting adventure, but there are sinister forces determined to keep her from acquiring the property.

Alain de Rochefort proves to be an enemy instead of the helpful friend he was supposed to be. Vesper finds herself locked in a car, shot at, and followed through the jungle by de Rochefort's henchmen. The girl meets the Chirica Indians who live in the dense jungle and are also threatened by de Rochefort. She is determined that their foes will not succeed in their evil intentions.

Vesper faces many dangers in the thick rain forest, but her courage never fails her, even when faced with imminent death.

The Beautiful Green Girl of the Rain Forest
A Mnemonic Story about Central America

There was once a girl whose family traveled south, all the way from Mexico to the deep, dark rain forest near the equator of Central America. Her name was Ellen, but everyone called her El. El was half-Indian and half-Spanish. People of this ancestry are called *mestizos*. Ellen was also very **beautiful**! El knew that her Spanish side came from her father, whose last name was Salvador. It is a very Spanish name.

El knew that the soldiers from Spain had come to her country many years before to find gold and other riches to send back to their king and country. Some of them were cruel and abused the native people. However, many of them stayed and married the Indian women because they loved the land and its culture. They brought their Spanish language and their Catholic religion to the new country. There was then a wonderful mixture of Spanish and Indian culture throughout the land.

These things didn't concern El at this time, however. She had a problem and wasn't sure she could solve it. It all started when she was a little girl and began to eat the plants in the rain forest. She was very careful to eat only the edible ones, but soon lost interest in any other kinds of food. El's mother warned her that if she persisted in eating nothing but the green plants, her skin would begin to take on a green color. El disregarded her mother's warnings, and over the years, the **beautiful** girl turned **green**!

El Salvador was not overly concerned about her unusual color until, at the age of eighteen, she met a very handsome man. El fell madly in love with this man, who always wore a wide-brimmed hat. It was called a Panama hat, and he wore it at all times. It was said that he even wore it to bed. People forgot his real name and just called him **Panama,** and they watched to see how he would respond to El.

Panama saw that El was a very **beautiful** girl, but he also saw that she was **green.**

"No way am I going to marry a green girl!" he said. And he began to run from her. Poor **El Salvador** ran after him. However, he got a head start, and El didn't have a chance. She **has never caught Panama.** To this day:

B-eautiful, G-reen El Salvador H-as N-ever C-aught P-anama!!

When you think of Central America, always remember **El Salvador,** who was **beautiful**, but **green!!** She fell in love and chased after him, but she **has never caught Panama!**

Beautiful Green El Salvador Has Never Caught Panama.

B for **Belize**

G for **Guatemala**

E for **El Salvador**

H for **Honduras**

N for **Nicaragua**

C for **Costa Rica**

P for **Panama**

These are the countries of Central America, in the order in which they are located from Mexico to South America. After saying the mnemonic sentence often enough, you will remember the names and locations of the countries—and some information about their history and culture, too!

From *Teaching Global Literacy Using Mnemonics* by Joan Ebbesmeyer.
Westport, CT: Libraries Unlimited/Teacher Ideas Press. Copyright © 2006.

Central America Activities: Remarkable Rain Forests

Research and Art (Standards 3, 7, 8, and 14)

Activity 1. The rain forests of Central America have four levels. They are the emergent layer, canopy, forest floor, and understory. If you can define *emergent, canopy, floor* and *understory,* you'll know where each layer is situated, from top to bottom. Now, try to draw a picture of the rain forest showing each layer.

Activity 2. Most of the trees of the rain forest are broadleaf and evergreen, but they belong to many different species. Many trees are associated with particular places in the world. What countries or areas of the world do you associate with the following trees? If some are unfamiliar, research them in an encyclopedia. In some cases, there is more than one correct answer.

1. Kapok
2. Joshua
3. Giant Sequoia
4. Banyon
5. Saguaro
6. Eucalyptus
7. Baobab
8. Palm
9. Traveler's Tree
10. Redwood

From *Teaching Global Literacy Using Mnemonics* by Joan Ebbesmeyer.
Westport, CT: Libraries Unlimited/Teacher Ideas Press. Copyright © 2006.

Activity: Did You Ever See a Poem Lovely as a Tree?

Fluency: Trees around the World (Standards 12–16)

List as many kinds of trees as you can think of.

_____ _____ _____

_____ _____ _____

_____ _____ _____

_____ _____ _____

Did you list the Ginkgo?

Enumerate all the ways that people use trees.

_____

_____

_____

_____

_____

_____

Did you remember they serve as Christmas trees?

What is the most unusual use for a tree that you found?

Did you think of the fact that a tree can be the inspiration for a poem? Find Joyce Kilmer's poem, "Trees." Memorize it.

List some of the products people get from trees.

_____ _____ _____

_____ _____ _____

_____ _____ _____

_____ _____ _____

Did you include acids?

Central America Activities: Amazing Analogies

Flexibility and Analogies (Standards 1–4)

To make analogies, you must decide how two items are related to each other and compare them with another relationship. The relationship can be similar, opposite, or parts of things. Think how the first two are compared before you form a new relationship.

Here's an example:

A <u>rain forest</u> is **compared to** a <u>canopy</u>, just **as** a <u>house</u> is compared to a _____?

The answer is <u>roof.</u>

When writing and reading analogies on this worksheet, know that the symbol "**:**" means "**compares to**" and "**::**" means "**as.**"

Try to figure out the following analogies about Central America.

1. Belize : (compares to the) English language :: (as) Costa Rica : _____

2. San Salvador : El Salvador :: Guatemala City : _____

3. Nicaragua : Cordoba :: Panama : _____

4. Humid : jungle :: dry : _____

5. Quinine : tree bark :: penicillin : _____

6. Jaguar : rain forest :: whale : _____

7. Three-toed sloth : Central America :: elephant : _____

8. Egypt : Suez :: Panama : _____

Now that you have learned about Mexico and Central America, how many analogies can you create concerning these countries? Exchange your analogies with other students to see if you can find the answers.

From *Teaching Global Literacy Using Mnemonics* by Joan Ebbesmeyer.
Westport, CT: Libraries Unlimited/Teacher Ideas Press. Copyright © 2006.

Central America Activities: Science

Plants and Sunlight (Standards 1, 7, and 8)

As you learn about the rain forest, you realize the effect that sunlight has on plants. The thick mass of foliage and trees are vying for the sunlight. The heat and moisture of the jungle produce thousands of plants reaching for the light of the sun.

For Lower-Level Students

Students can see how plants will find light by building a simple plant maze.

1. Students will need a sprouting potato, placed in a pot of soil, with the sprout above the dirt.
2. Have students place the pot in one side of a cardboard box. On the other side, have them *carefully* cut a round hole.
3. Students fix a wall between the potato and the hole and close the box tightly. Open it daily. Water lightly. Watch the sprout seek the light!

Assessment Ideas

There are many ways to assess student learning other than tests and written reports.

- Students enjoy holding *Quiz Bowls*. Teams are drawn up to create their own questions on the information they research and learn about Mexico and Central America. Teams compete against each other, and the winners can receive small rewards.

- A *Book of Rhymes* can be created about the region students are studying. The rhymes are simple, four-line clues about the subject area.

Example:

Central American Countries
I am a country,
That begins with a "B."
I'm just south of Mexico.
Can you name me?

Students may want to create additional rhyming clues and present them to other classes.

- Students can work in pairs or groups to create *Clue Question Games* for the people, places and things they have learned about Mexico and Central America. It can be a contest. (Five points for an answer after first clue; four points after second clue, and so on.)

Examples
Clue 1.

1. I am a very mountainous country in Central America.
2. I have about 3.5 million people living in me.
3. I have the most stable government in Central America.
4. I am located between Nicaragua and Panama.

5. My capital is San Jose.

The name of the country is _____.

Clue 2.
1. Some of my species are threatened by jungle loss.
2. I make very loud noises that can be heard for miles.
3. I am among the most intelligent creatures on earth.
4. I swing from tree to tree.
5. I howl!

What am I?

Now you try one!
1. I am a Mayan ruin.
2. _____
3. _____
4. _____
5. _____

What is my name?

1. I am the only country in Central America that does not touch the Atlantic Ocean.
2. _____
3. _____
4. _____
5. _____

Which country am I?

Answers for Mexico and Central America

Remarkable Rain Forests, Activity 2 (p. 50)

1. South America
2. Desert
3. California
4. India
5. Mexico
6. Australia
7. Africa
8. Florida
9. Madagascar
10. California

Flexibility and Analogies (p. 52)

1. Spanish
2. Guatemala
3. Balboa
4. desert
5. mold
6. ocean
7. Africa
8. Panama Canal

Assessment Ideas: Clue Game (pp. 53–54)

Clue 1. Costa Rica

Clue 2. Howler Monkey

Mexico

Suggested Reading

Picture Book

O'Dell, Scott. *The Treasure of Topo-El-Bampo.* Illustrated by Lynd Ward. Houghton Mifflin Company, 1972.

 The wealth of Mexico comes from the land. There are three areas that provide this wealth: the fertile valleys, the mountains, and the deep earth and wells.

 This book tells of the mountain wealth—silver—that was stolen by the Spanish for many, many years and sent to enrich the king and country of Spain.

 The setting is Topo El Bampo, the poorest village in Mexico. It is hard to imagine how hard these people had to work to keep themselves from starvation. Even the mayor was poor—so poor he had to sell his two small burros to the Spanish mine owners who were sending all the silver to the Spanish king who ruled Mexico at that time.

 What the two burros did while they traveled across country with the silver bars on their back makes a wonderfully sensitive story, and it turned Topo El Bampo into the richest village in Mexico.

Chapter Book

Paulsen, Gary. *The Crossing.* Orchard Books, 1987.

 Few children can imagine what life is like when you have no parents, no home but a cardboard box, and must fight every day just to survive. Manuel Bustos was one child who lived that life. He was born in a Mexican border town and lived on the streets as he yearned to reach the "promised land" of America that lay so near, and yet so far.

 The night he took the chance to cross the muddy Rio Grande illegally was the night he met the Vietnam War veteran Sergeant Locke, who would change his life forever. Sergeant Locke was not the enemy, but Manny found many dangers on the streets of the American border town, the greatest being the street wolves!

 Manny desperately needed someone to befriend him, but he never expected there was anyone willing to lay down his life for him.

Mexico: Activities

Research and Creative Writing (Standards 7, 9, 10, and 17)

Remember the great ancient civilizations of Mexico by chanting a mnemonic rhyme:

> The four great cultures
> There's no denyin'
> Were Olmecs, Toltecs,
> Aztecs, and Mayan!

- Research one of the ancient cultures and make up a rhyme or short story about it.

- Draw a picture of an ancient Mayan or Aztec city. Include the great stone temples and pyramids. The school library will have many picture books to give students ideas. Don't forget the Aztec altar for human sacrifice.

Spanish Language

The Spanish ruled Mexico for centuries. They stripped the country of its wealth and defeated the indigenous (native) people who had no firearms. Although the natives had been skilled mathematicians, astronomers, craftsmen, and musicians, they were left poverty-stricken.

- If you learn some basic Spanish, you will understand the meanings of geographic locations. For example:

    Sierra means "mountain." *Madre* means "mother." Imagine the great mountain ranges that extend the length of Mexico's east and west sides as mother's arms that embrace the great plateau between them. This could help you remember why they might have called their mountain ranges "Mountain Mother."

    Rio means "river." *Grande* means "great." What is it? Where do you find it?

    Mexico has two important peninsulas (land surrounded by water on three sides). Cancun is a well-known resort area on one of them, the Yucatan. It juts out into the Gulf of Mexico, below Florida. Think of the many people who flock there for the beach and hot sun. Remembering "You can tan in the Yucatan" will help you remember the name. The other peninsula is called Baja (pronounced "bah-hah") California. Why do you think California is part of the name? Is it because of its location? Can you think of a mnemonic to remember this peninsula?

- Study the map of Mexico that follows and see how many of the following locations you can find and label.

Sierra Madre Mountains	Rio Grande River
Yucatan Peninsula	Baja California
Gulf of Mexico	Gulf of California

Can you label other important locations? Where is the capital city, Mexico City, located?

58   Teaching Global Literacy Using Mnemonics

Mexico

From *Teaching Global Literacy Using Mnemonics* by Joan Ebbesmeyer.
Westport, CT: Libraries Unlimited/Teacher Ideas Press. Copyright © 2006.

Chapter 3

Canada

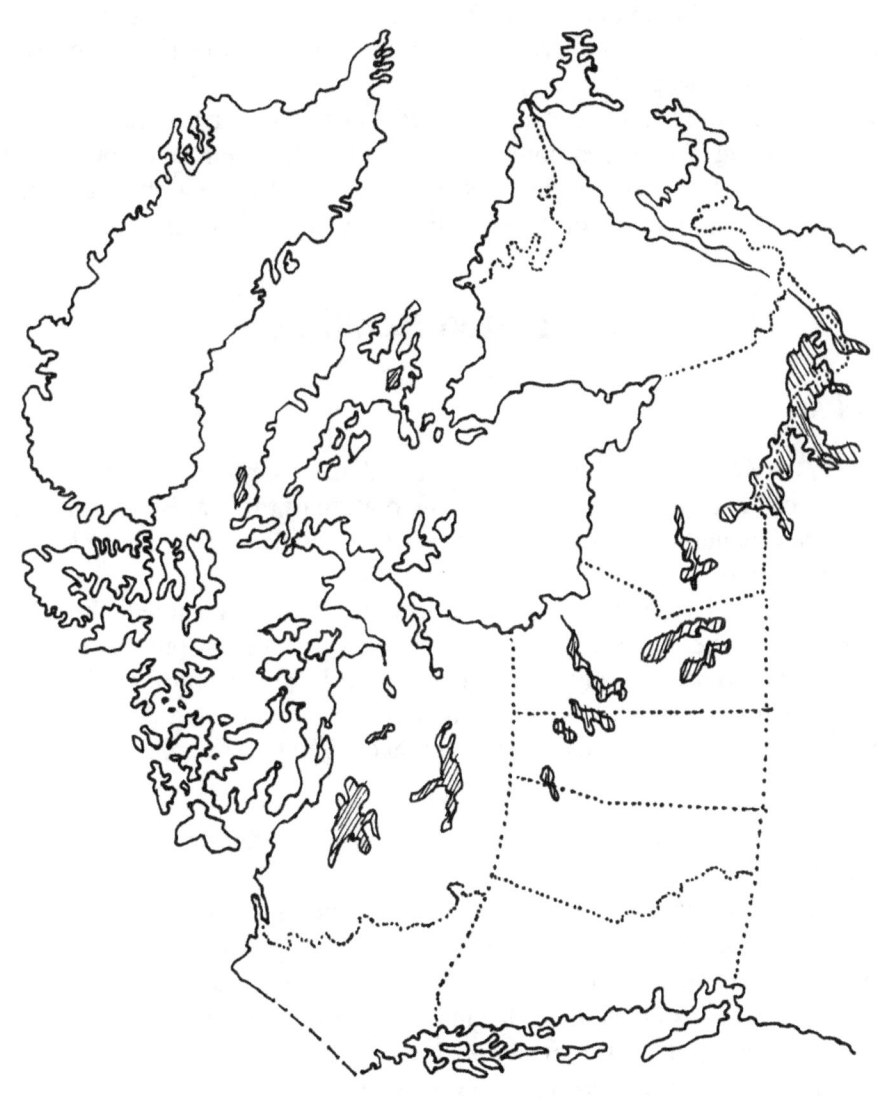

Canada

America's neighbor country to the north is the world's second largest nation—and also one of the least populated. The population is so small in this spacious land that stretches from the Atlantic to the Pacific Ocean because much of it is covered with ice and snow. However, it is rich in many natural resources and is a friendly trading partner with the United States. Students need to become more familiar with the history, geography, and importance of this great and exciting ally that shares a common border of nearly four thousand miles. It is the world's longest continuous border between two nations.

Americans and Canadians need to know each other well and to remain steadfast in their friendship and respect for each other. It is difficult to like or respect someone you do not know, yet few American students are even aware that Canada is divided into provinces and territories.

Teachers need to find an incentive to stimulate interest in learning more about our neighbor to the north. There are excellent picture and chapter books that can provide this motivation. Storytelling of the exciting exploits of the early Canadian explorers, such as Henry Hudson, Jacques Cartier, Samuel Champlain, and Father Marquette, the bloody wars between the French and English nations, and the brutal Iroquois Indians who tried to drive out explorers and missionaries alike, are great ways to excite student interest in Canada.

In addition, there are the courageous and talented North American Indians known as the Haida (pronounced "HI-da") and Tlingit (pronounced "TLING-git"). Their ceremonial potlatch parties, carved boats, and totem poles are interesting to learn about. The Yukon with its gold rush stories and the Northwest Territory with its tales of the Canadian Mounted Police just add to the fun.

Suggested Reading

Picture Books

Adams, Jan. *Very Last First Time.* Illustrated by Ian Wallace. Margaret K. McElderry, 1985.

Few of us can even imagine walking on the bottom of the sea. But if you can find Ungava Bay in northern Canada, you'll know where the Inuit people do just that to find mussels to eat during the wintertime.

This story tells of Eva, an Inuit girl who is lowered through the hole in the ice to stand on the bottom of the sea. It is her first time gathering mussels while the tide pulls the sea from the shore.

Eva is excited to see this mysterious new world by the candles she has placed between rocks. The tide pools, anemones, and seaweed fascinate her, but when she hears the sea returning and her candles blow out, Eva finds herself in great danger. Can she make it back to the exit hole in time?

Dixon, Ann (reteller). *How Raven Brought Light to People.* Illustrated by James Watts. Macmillan, 1992.

In this ancient Indian myth, Raven the trickster knows that the chief has three beautifully carved chests he uses for important ceremonies to fill with valuable gifts for his guests. The chief, above all others, must show off his wealth and prove his important position in the tribe, by owning priceless things. Raven knows that in these chests are the sun, moon, and stars. Because the earth is still in darkness, Raven must find a way to trick the chief into giving him the "chests of light"! He succeeds in his trickery, but he pays a big price.

London, Jonathan. *The Sugaring-Off Party.* Paintings by Giles Polluter. RosterButton Children's Books, 1995.

> This delightfully illustrated book is all about tradition—in particular, traditions that the people of French descent who live in the province of Quebec hold almost sacred.
>
> Paul listens to his grandmother relating how the families have gathered for years to celebrate the coming of spring, by boiling the maple sap down into sugar. It's called a sugaring-off party and involves a great gathering of people, who eat and dance and finally partake of the delicious maple-candy treat. When it's over, the friends and family disperse to return home to sleep and dream of the next year's sugar-moon celebration.

Parson, Nan. *The Way Home.* RosterButton Children's Books, 1999.

> An injured Canadian goose is lucky when Samuel and his father find her as they walk by the large pond on their farm. Father doesn't have much hope for the goose, but he and the boy nurse her back to health, with the gander watching and waiting close by. Samuel learns much about geese before the goose and her mate fly away to their summer home. The last thing he learns is how to let go of those you love, when the right time comes. Samuel is rewarded.

Chapter Books

Anderson, Margaret J. *The Journey of the Shadow Barns.* Alfred K. Knopf, 1980.

> Thirteen-year-old Elspeth and her four-year-old brother travel from Scotland to Canada against all odds. The two were left orphaned, and all that was left to them were one-way tickets to another world across the ocean and a small amount of money.
>
> Elspeth knows the authorities will not let them travel alone, but she is determined they will not be separated and will fulfill their father's dream of finding a home in the province of Saskatchewan. The two children must become "shadow barns" and hide from immigration officials and police to succeed in their venture. They face disease, robbery, and harsh conditions of an alien land, but they also find kindness and help from unexpected sources. This is a story of courage—the kind found in Canadian immigrants.

Buchanan, Dawn Lisa. *The Falcon's Wing.* A Richard Jackson Book, 1992.

> Life changes completely for Bern when her father uproots her from the home she has always known in Ohio and moves her to a country village in the province of Ontario, Canada.
>
> Wasn't it enough that she had lost her mother? Now she faces living with an elderly aunt and cousin Wine, who has Down syndrome. There is also the terror of the Castor River.
>
> Bern finds no warmth or understanding from her father and Aunt Pearl until her cousin Wine unlocks the secrets and brings about new closeness and understanding to the whole family.

Two Countries—One Nation
Mnemonic Story about the Ten Provinces of Canada

There was once a boy, named John, who lived in Nova Scotia, one of Canada's four Atlantic provinces, named because they border the Atlantic Ocean. John felt very proud that he was named after John Cabot, the great explorer who claimed this cold, vast land for Great Britain. Cabot made his claim only five years after Columbus discovered America. John believed firmly that when you think "Canada," you think **British!**

However, his best friend Jacques had quite different feelings about their country. He lived in the province of Quebec and thought of Canada as French. Jacques was named after Jacques Cartier, the explorer who had sailed the St. Lawrence River so many years ago and claimed the land now called Quebec for France.

This difference of opinion was threatening to ruin their friendship until they both attended a high school class that made them think with new perspectives (viewpoints).

Their history teacher taught them about the time of the great explorations when the nations of Europe were looking for new routes and waterways to the East, where they hoped to find wealth to bring back to their own countries.

Great Britain was the European island-country surrounded by oceans. It had watched Portugal and France claim lands in the New World. The Britons decided that as *always,* they had better *sail quickly* to *name new nations permanently* for themselves. There were many exciting stories of adventure about the English and French explorers. The boys realized now that both countries and many brave men had worked, fought, and created this great nation of Indian, French, and English cultures. They learned about the diversity (positive differences) of the people and culture of Canada's ten provinces and two territories and how these differences added to the strength of their country, through unification. The boys decided it was similar to the unification of the 50 U.S. states.

The two great territories, the Yukon and the vast Northwest Territory, that stretched across the entire northern part of the Canadian arctic regions added to their pride and awe in the second largest country in the world! Only Russia was larger. Both boys had a new appreciation for the value of the mixed cultures of their country.

In the end, it was the **Britons,** who **always sailed** the **many oceans** that surrounded their country. They did it **quickly, naming new nations** before the French could claim them, and holding the new lands **permanently** for Great Britain. Canada is still connected to Great Britain to this day! This is because:

Britons Always Sailed Many Oceans Quickly Naming New Nations Permanently!

B for **British Columbia**

A for **Alberta**

S for **Saskatchewan**

M for **Manitoba**

O for **Ontario**

Q for **Quebec**

From *Teaching Global Literacy Using Mnemonics* by Joan Ebbesmeyer. Westport, CT: Libraries Unlimited/Teacher Ideas Press. Copyright © 2006.

N for **Newfoundland**

N for **Nova Scotia**

N for **New Brunswick**

P for **Prince Edward Island**

When you think of Canada, think *British*. It will help you remember how to start the mnemonic sentence, "Britons always sailed many oceans quickly, naming new nations permanently."

You will then know the ten provinces of Canada and where they are located in sequence, from the western coast of the Pacific to the eastern Atlantic coastal region. The ten provinces are bordered on the north by the two territories, the Yukon and the Northwest Territory, in addition to many arctic islands. The story you just read reveals names, locations, and some of Canada's history.

Canada Activities: Hail to the Haida

Research (Standards 2, 4, 6, 10, and 18)

The Haida Indians are an interesting research topic looking into the history and culture of parts of Canada and Alaska. These people were great seagoing and woodcarving natives of the vast western-coast regions of the north. Their art was shown in the beautifully carved ceremonial chests, the decorated prows of their boats, and their tall totem poles. They lived in long, wooden houses, decorated inside and out with intricate carvings. The people were wealthy and talented, with a fascinating way of life!

1. After researching the Haida and other native tribes of Canada, write a short paragraph patterned on *The Important Book* by Margaret Wise Brown (HarperTrophy, 1990; originally published in 1949). It is a simple book, listing the important things about a subject and ending with what the writer considers the *most* important thing.

Example: John Cabot

The important things about John Cabot were:

1. He was an Italian, but he sailed as an explorer for England.
2. He was the first European since the Vikings to visit Canada.
3. He sailed along the coast of Newfoundland in 1497.
4. He claimed Canada for England just five years after Columbus discovered America.
5. Cabot's claim to Canada was thirty-seven years before Cartier's claim for France.

But *the most important thing* about John Cabot was:

He gave England a claim to part of North America, which led to the formation of the first English colonies.

Canada Activities: Analyze with Attributes

Analysis: Attribute Thinking (Standards 2–4, 6)

The Inuit people of northern Canada are native to the land. They have similar needs to the people of all cultures. They differ in the qualities they develop to provide those needs and survive the harsh conditions of the region where they live. All cultures, regions, and ways of life demand certain qualities to live successfully. People who live in the desert, the mountains, or the arctic regions must develop qualities, characteristics, and attributes that are unique to their way of life.

After learning about the Inuit people of the Arctic regions, show how different their characteristics are by creating a definition by attributes. List the attributes evidenced by these native people. Use them to define "Inuit."

Physical Attributes	Social Attributes	Mental Attributes

Example: Creating a Definition Paragraph

List qualities:

1. Physical qualities: tiny, soft, cute, fragile
2. Social qualities: cooing, crying, demanding, babbling
3. Mental qualities: clinging, searching, learning, growing
4. Other: sleeping, eating, wet, hungry

Now use the words to write a "Definition Paragraph":

This is a tiny, soft, helpless mass of humanity, turning a whole family into eager servants with one demanding cry. A "coo" and a "goo" and a babble, like a small lilting brook, that can quickly change to a shriek and smell bad, while clinging like a little animal when hungry, lonely, or wet. An endless eating and growing, searching and grabbing being, who finally sleeps and creates the image of a fragile, innocent, heart-catching member of human society.

This is the Definition of a Baby.

As you study the different peoples of the world, their characteristics and qualities become evident. They depend on the environment in which they live. The desert Bedouins of northern Africa and Yanomami Indians of South America living in the rain forest are different in many ways, just as native Australian Aborigines are different from a resident of New York City. Even so, they all have some unique characteristics.

Listing the different qualities can provide a lot of information about many people and areas of the world.

Canada Activities: Potlatch Party

Economics: Critical Thinking, Problem Solving (Standards 10, 11, 14, and 15)

All cultures have a system of economics. They find a way to use their resources to meet their needs and wants. It may be as simple as bartering (trading) or as complex as capitalism (the United States system).

An economic system began in the Indian tribes of British Columbia by having lavish parties called a potlatch. The host gained great prestige by giving expensive gifts to his guests, who gave even more expensive gifts in return at the next potlatch. The gifts were kept in beautifully carved chests made by native artists. These expensive gifts could be used for bartering between families or individuals.

In some ways, little has changed in how we show our wealth and economic power. Many people still try to "keep up with the Joneses"!

Compare the Canadian Indian's wealth to today's adults and to what you consider economically powerful.

Potlatch Power	Power for Today's Adults	What You Consider Wealth
Carved statues	Mercedes	Nike shoes
Goat-hair blankets	Harley-Davidson motorcycle	Computer
Copper plates	Indoor pool	Sports car

Add as many things as you can to the lists, and then think of the problems that might arise in school-age young people from gaining economic power through expensive clothes, cars, jewelry, and other material things. One might be even jealousy. List others.

Work in groups and decide which, in your opinion, is the most important problem with gaining too much affluence for school-age youngsters. Follow the problem-solving steps to see if you can find a solution.

1. State the most important problem.

2. What vital information do you have concerning this problem?

3. Decide on three possible solutions to the problem.

4. Which criteria will you use to judge your solutions?

(Example: too dangerous, too expensive, inspires friendship, helps people cooperate)

5. Do your judging and select the best solution!

Problem solving can be practiced in considering many historical Canadian events.

Consider the great Yukon gold rush, when thousands of men lost everything, sometimes their lives, in a mad search for sudden wealth. Could they have become rich in other ways in the Yukon? How about opening a laundry for all those men?

Think of Henry Hudson, courageous enough to make four trips across the ocean to reach the Orient. His men mutinied on the last voyage and set him adrift in a small boat amid the wilds of the Arctic. Could they have reached their goal of going back home in another way? Could they have asked for a democratic vote?

How has Canada solved the problem of keeping Quebec, a province dedicated to its French roots, united with the rest of the country?

Literature Activity: Classics (Standards 5 and 6)

There are some great classic books, poems, and stories about the regions of Canada and the Arctic. Jack London's exciting stories such as "To Build a Fire" and his famous books, *Call of the Wild* and *White Fang,* will never grow old.

Robert Service wrote a great, funny story-poem, called *The Cremation of Sam McGee,* about what could happen to those men who tried to find gold in the frigid North. Service and London were both successful writers who loved the Arctic lands and got caught up in what Service called, "the spell of the Yukon." However, their real lives were very dissimilar. Students could learn of the authors' lives by comparing and contrasting the commonalties and differences of their backgrounds and the ways they lived their lives.

Canada Activities: Magnificent Metaphors

Authors: Creative Writing and Metaphoric Thinking (Standards 9 and 10)

Many of Jack London's stories were about the bond of friendship between humans and dogs. The Yukon in the 1840s demanded great trust and loyalty between the two if they were to survive. These stories are a good lead-in for thinking and writing in metaphor. Think of a metaphor for their favorite animal or pet. This will encourage you to compare an animal to an inanimate object that has common attributes, or characteristics. These metaphors can be expanded to phrases and sentences and serve as story starters. Examples follow. Create metaphors for the remaining animals.

Animal	Metaphor
White Fang	A symbol of freedom
Sloth	
Cat	
Turtle	A domed antique
Canary	
Lion	
Horse	
Seal	
Mouse	
Snake	Ribbon of fear

Expanding into Phrases

- White Fang: A symbol of freedom in the wilderness
- Turtle: A domed antique in the vast desert
- Snake: A ribbon of fear in the murky water

Expanding into Sentences

- The fearless White Fang was a symbol of freedom as he prowled the endless wilderness of the Yukon Territory.
- The slow and plodding turtle is a domed antique. It survives harsh conditions when countless other animals succumb to the perils of the desert.
- The weaving anaconda snake is a ribbon of fear that moves through the murky waters of the Amazon.

From *Teaching Global Literacy Using Mnemonics* by Joan Ebbesmeyer.
Westport, CT: Libraries Unlimited/Teacher Ideas Press. Copyright © 2006.

Use the research you have done on the animals of the region of the world you are studying to create exciting and original sentences filled with descriptive words, metaphors, similes, and alliteration. These figures of speech can be expanded into paragraphs and finally into stories about unique places, peoples, and animals that can be found in the vast regions of Canada. It can improve your creative writing and make it more interesting to read. Fill in the metaphors and expansions that follow.

Animals of Canada Metaphor Expansion

1. The grizzly bear is a dark nightmare as he rises on his back legs and lifts his dangerous clawed hands in defiance!

2. The migrating caribou

3. The graceful crane is a study in grace as she slowly lifts herself into the sky.

4. The howling wolf

5. The lumbering moose

6. The magnificent eagle

7. The soaring waxwing

8. The fur-bearing beaver

9. The darting lynx

10. The persevering sled-dog

Canada Activities: Tell Your Totem

Art: Characteristics (Standards 14–16)

The artwork of the original people of Canada was influenced by their family histories, the animals of the region, their age-old legends, and the beauty of nature that touched every part of their great land.

The Haida totem poles were carved to tell stories of the owner's family history. They depicted animals, stories, and personal dreams and accomplishments of the family.

Use the drawing of a totem pole that follows. Draw one next to it, or on a separate sheet, and fill it in to tell the story of your family. You may have to talk to parents, grandparents, and other family members to gather background information. Let your totem pole tell of your family interests and accomplishments.

From *Teaching Global Literacy Using Mnemonics* by Joan Ebbesmeyer.
Westport, CT: Libraries Unlimited/Teacher Ideas Press. Copyright © 2006.

Canada Activities: Pretty Pottery

All cultures show their aesthetic (artistic) abilities in their drawings, paintings, sculpture, and architecture. The early Indians of Canada found beauty in nature, portraying it on pottery and ceremonial masks.

Think of mountains and rivers, flowers and trees, the sun and the stars as you design and decorate the pottery below. You may want your pictographs to tell a story.

Indian Pottery

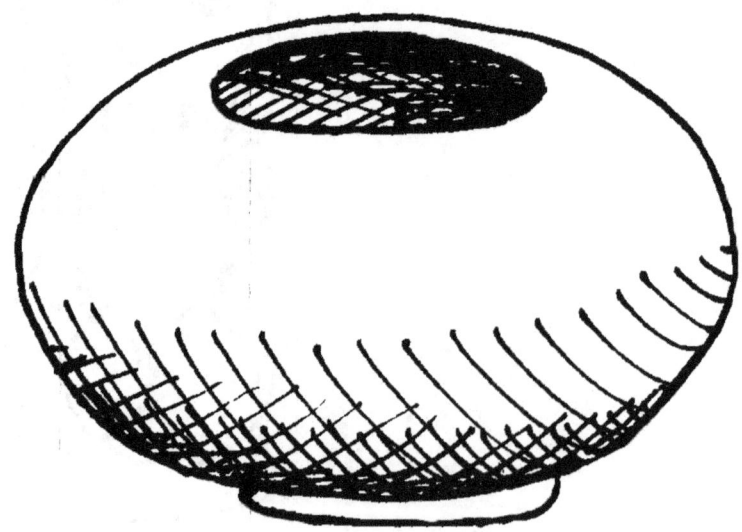

From *Teaching Global Literacy Using Mnemonics* by Joan Ebbesmeyer.
Westport, CT: Libraries Unlimited/Teacher Ideas Press. Copyright © 2006.

Canada Activities: People Wear Many Masks

Masks are used in every culture on earth and for many kinds of ceremonies. The Indians of Canada used masks, too. The first mask below was used by Indian medicine men to cure sick persons. Create other masks and tell what ceremonies they were used for.

From *Teaching Global Literacy Using Mnemonics* by Joan Ebbesmeyer.
Westport, CT: Libraries Unlimited/Teacher Ideas Press. Copyright © 2006.

Canada Activities:
The Great Lakes of the United States and Canada
A Mnemonic Story about the Great Lakes

Billy grew up in the state of Michigan and was proud of how unique it was. He noticed on the map that it was shaped like a big mitten and was surrounded by water on three sides. That made it a peninsula! It was the only state made up of *two* peninsulas—an upper and a lower one, connected by a five-mile bridge.

Billy understood why thousands of tourists came every year to see the four Great Lakes that bordered his state. (Lake Ontario is the only one that doesn't touch Michigan.) The tourists came to see the largest group of fresh-water lakes in the world! These lakes are the most important inland waterway in North America. Billy was very proud! And even though there were thousands and thousands of other lakes in his state, he never tired of looking at the water because he loved to swim more than anything else in the world. He swam in every pool, pond, lake, or ocean that his parents allowed him to dive into. He also liked football, soccer, and movies. He actually enjoyed everything. Everything, that is, except **onions**! He **hated onions!** He hated them as much as he loved swimming. That's why he had to eat onions if he ever broke an important family rule.

Billy never forgot the rule until the summer he traveled to Michigan's Upper Peninsula with his parents. He had been forbidden to swim in the greatest of all lakes, Lake Superior. Mother said it was too dangerous, and she was right.

Billy resisted temptation until the last day of vacation. Then he decided he just had to swim in that beautiful lake that looked as large as an ocean. He plunged into the water, swam gloriously for a short while, and climbed out to see his mother's angry face peering at him. Of course, you know what happened next!!

She Made Him Eat Onions!

Remember this sentence and use the first letters of each word to help you remember the Great Lakes, largest to smallest, and west to east:

S for **Superior**

M for **Michigan**

H for **Huron**

E for **Erie**

O for **Ontario**

Chapter 4
South America

South America

South America is the great triangle-shaped continent that lies south of Central America and between the Atlantic and Pacific Oceans. The towering Andes Mountains reach from the north to the south along the western coast of the continent. The northeastern area is covered by dense rain forest, and the south has great open plains of scrub and grasslands.

Despite the potential for great wealth in mineral resources and farmlands, many of the twelve countries on the continent remain very poor. Less than two hundred years ago, most of South America was ruled by Spain and Portugal, creating a population of European descendants, natives, and people of mixed ancestry. When independence from colonial rule was finally gained by the twelve countries, unstable governments were the result. The great and ancient Incan Empire was literally destroyed by Spanish invasion and rule.

The Spanish and Portuguese had a lasting influence on the language and religion, but today's South American countries are independent and working to develop industries to take advantage of their natural resources and overcome the poverty that persists in many parts of the continent.

Suggested Reading

Picture Books

Cherry, Lynne. *The Great Kapoc Tree*. Harcourt Brace, 1990.

Strange things begin to happen as a man tries to chop down the great Kapoc tree that grows in the Amazon rain forest. When the man takes a nap in the heat of the day, the boa constrictor slithers down to hiss a message into his ear. The monkey, tree frog, anteater, and toucan have their own information to add. Even the mighty jaguar, the slow-moving sloth, and the Yanomami Indian boy communicate their desperate plea to the sleeping man.

When the man awakes, he looks at the tree in a whole new light. He sees all the creatures—plants, animals, and people—that depend on the tree for their survival. He can no longer play a part in the destruction of this wonderful world!

Lester, Alison. *Isabella's Bed*. Houghton Mifflin, 1993.

This simple story tells of the mysterious bed and sandalwood chest from South America in the attic of Grandmother's house. The two grandchildren love to find the many treasures that fill the chest, but Grandmother will never tell them anything about her past until the night they sleep in the bed and all their exciting dreams reveal the great mountains, deserts, rivers, and waterfalls of that vast continent. The dream brings a change in Grandmother's heart, and she begins to tell her story.

Torres, Leyla. *Saturday Sancocho*. Farrar, Straus & Giroux, 1995.

Maria Lili lives in South America. She visits the rural farm of her grandparents every Saturday to help prepare and eat chicken sancocho with them. One Saturday, the family has no money to buy the ingredients for the stew. All they have are a dozen eggs. Grandmother thinks of a way to use the eggs to get all the vegetables and chicken they need. As Maria Lili watches, she learns about the value of bartering, an economic strategy from earliest times that is still in use today.

Chapter Books

Ellis, Ella Thorp. *Roam the Wild Country.* Atheneum, 1967.
    This is a great story of the vast regions of Argentina and the South American cowboys, called gauchos who roam the wild country on their magnificent horses. Martin is only thirteen years old when he becomes a horse breaker. It is the dream of a lifetime, but the drought has brought about a lack of the pampas grass needed to keep the horses from starvation. Martin and the other young gauchos have to lead the horses over the high Andean mountains in search of food—a nearly impossible job!

Griffiths, Helen. *Stallion of the Sands.* Lothrop, Lee & Shepard, 1968.
    The wild-riding gauchos (cowboys) of the vast, open grassy plains called the pampas can make an exciting tale when coupled with a proud, strong, free albino stallion. Aurelio is just a boy, but he decides to join the gauchos and learn to ride the plains of Argentina and herd the roaming cattle.
    The boy and the stallion meet in the land of mists, and there he finds the answer to riddles and the fulfillment of a dream.

Smith, Roland. *Jaguar.* Hyperion Books for Children, 1997.
    This story has all the elements of adventure, as Jake Lanza finally gets to leave his home in New York to meet his father in the mysterious, lush Amazon rain forest of Brazil. He looks forward to helping his father set up a jaguar preserve in the jungle, but he has no idea of the dangers that he must face as tragedy destroys their boat and he witnesses death for the first time.
    Jake grows up fast as he endures many conflicts and life-threatening experiences. In the end, it is a matter of survival!

Anna Learns a New Alphabet
A Mnemonic Story about South America

Anna was on her way from her home in Alaska to travel the length of two continents and spend a month with Grandfather Mendez in Argentina. Grandfather was a gaucho (a South American cowboy) who rode and roped horses on a large cattle ranchero on the vast, open, grassy plains called the pampas. Anna would be gone for a month during the school term, and the one condition for being absent that long was to teach her classmates about Argentina and the continent of South America on her return.

Anna did not take this responsibility lightly. She paid close attention to all the scenes and experiences she encountered in South America as she traveled from the busy port of Caracas, Venezuela, in the far north, to Argentina at the southern tip of the continent. Anna studied a map and noticed that South America was shaped like a cone with a large scoop of ice cream at the top. As she journeyed south, she saw the majestic Andes Mountains to her right and the amazing Amazon River and rain forest to her left. She was aware that everyone spoke either Spanish or Portuguese because those countries had ruled most of South America. Some countries gained independence in the nineteenth century, others not until the twentieth century. One part of South America, French Guiana, is still controlled by a European country, France.

Anna felt it most important that her classmates know the names and locations of the countries. She decided to use the first five letters of the alphabet to remember the countries on the western side of the continent.

It was a silly alphabet. Instead of A-B-C-D-E, it became **A-B-C-*P*-E.** Starting at the southernmost country with Argentina, the letters stood for:

A for **Argentina**

B for **Bolivia and Brazil**

C for **Columbia and Chile**

P for **Peru**

E for **Ecuador**

Anna created a story to tell about the remaining countries of South America and some of the astounding facts she learned on her trips across the continent. Her story goes like this:

There is a famous set of twins living in South America, named Paraguay and Uruguay. Paraguay's name starts with a P because she is a prisoner and landlocked along with her neighbor, Bolivia. Uruguay, who lives on the beautiful Atlantic coastline, feels sorry for his imprisoned twin and makes up exciting stories of the different regions and countries to cheer her. He told her of the three little "**guys**" who lived next to each other on the northern coast. They were called "**Guy**" ana, French "**Gui**" ana (still a region belonging to France), and "**Sur**" (SIR) inam. Paraguay laughed at his play on words and begged him to tell her more. Uruguay told her about the "Venice of South America," Venezuela, so named by the first explorers because the watery lands reminded them of the Italian city of Venice in Europe.

From *Teaching Global Literacy Using Mnemonics* by Joan Ebbesmeyer.
Westport, CT: Libraries Unlimited/Teacher Ideas Press. Copyright © 2006.

Paraguay had heard about the silly alphabet, A B C P E, and now, with all the added stories, she knew all the countries of the continent. She could remember the entire thirteen members (twelve countries and one French region) of the South American family.
They were: **A, B, C, P, E**

Argentina, Bolivia, Brazil, Colombia, Chile, Peru, Ecuador

"Guay twins": Para**(guay)** and Uru**(guay)**

"Three guys": **Guyana, French Guiana,** ("SIR") **Surinam**

Venice: **(Venez)uela.**

However, Uruguay wasn't finished with entertaining Paraguay about the wonders of this interesting continent. So he gave her a little riddle in rhyme:

Can you find the largest, can you find the highest?

Can you find the longest, can you find the driest?

They all start with an "A"!!

Paraguay was mystified until Uruguay told her of the five wonders of South America!

A for **Amazon River and the Amazon rain forest** (the largest river and rain forest in the world)

A for **Angel Falls** (the highest waterfall in the world)

A for **Andes Mountains** (the longest mountain range in the world)

A for **Atacoma** (the driest desert in the world)

Paraguay was proud to be a part of such a great and wonderful continent!

South America Activities: Equator—Earth's Circle

Research, Science, and Map Use (Standards 1, 2, 4–8, 16, and 18)

Much of South America is tropical rain forest. These forests are hot, humid, and lie near the equator. They can be found in parts of Africa, Asia, Central America, South America, and on islands of the Pacific Ocean. These forests have more species of plants and animals than anywhere else on Earth. Trees can grow two hundred feet high, and treasure is found in timber, food, and the medicine these trees can produce.

Earth cannot survive without the rain forests. South America has the largest one—the Amazon!

Look at the map of the world below. Use your atlas and draw a solid line across the area of the equator. To give you an idea of the location of the world's rain forests, draw dotted lines locating the Tropic of Cancer and the Tropic of Capricorn. Then shade in the rain forest areas in Central America, South America, Africa, and Asia.

From *Teaching Global Literacy Using Mnemonics* by Joan Ebbesmeyer.
Westport, CT: Libraries Unlimited/Teacher Ideas Press. Copyright © 2006.

South America Activities: Trees, Trees Everywhere

Compare and Contrast: Regions of the World (Standards 1, 2, 4–8, 16, and 18)

The story of the Kapoc tree is a vivid and visual reminder of the importance of plant and animal life in the rain forest. It shows their interdependence and relationship to each other and reminds us of the same human connection—like plants and animals, people depend on each other.

The Kapoc tree is associated with South America, and the Baobab tree is associated with Africa. Many trees are associated with the region where they are found on Earth.

Activity 1. Connect the list of trees to the regions or countries where they are found.

Trees	Regions
Giant Sequoia	Madagascar (African country)
Ombu tree	California (USA)
Saguaro	Sonoran Desert (USA)
Banyon tree	India
Traveler's tree	Argentina

Activity 2. More than 2,500 kinds of trees can be found in the rain forests of South America. Work in groups or pairs to research and find how many trees you can list, from A to Z.

A	B	C Cassava	D
E	F	G	H
I	J	K	L
M	N	O	P Portulaca
Q Quebracho	R	S	T
U	V	W	X
Y	Z		

From *Teaching Global Literacy Using Mnemonics* by Joan Ebbesmeyer.
Westport, CT: Libraries Unlimited/Teacher Ideas Press. Copyright © 2006.

Activity 3. The main land regions of South America are:

1. Andes Mountains
2. Central Plains
3. Rain Forests

In all these areas you can find many animals. Almost *one-fourth of all known animals* can be found in South America. Think of the three habitats of South America and study the list below to learn where you would find them:

M for **Mountains**

P for **Plains**

R for **Rain Forests**

Llama ____	Jaguar ____	Guanaco ____
Giant Sloth ____	Sapajou Monkey ____	Coypu Rat ____
Condor ____	Puma ____	Vicuna ____
Swamp Deer P___	Toucan ____	Alpaca ____
Rhea ____	Boa Constrictor ____	Capybara R___

South America Activities: Magical Metaphors

Metaphoric Thinking: Creative and Critical Thinking

Thinking in metaphor is the ability to see the similarity between two very different things.

Activity 1. In the book *The Great Kapoc Tree,* we find a rain forest full of animals, people, objects, and concepts that can be part of a metaphor. It takes some creative and critical thinking, but as you study the wonders of the jungle—what they look like, what they do, their importance, their goals, and what they are made of—you may begin to see similarities between the rain forest and other, seemingly very different things.

Examples

1. How is the rain forest like an apartment house?

2. How is an anaconda like a steel ribbon?

3. How are the trees of the rain forest like lungs?

4. How is a jungle parrot like a rainbow?
   Both are very beautiful. Both are rather rare and colorful. Both are usually seen from on high.

5. How is the Amazon River like a snake?

To think in metaphor, you must practice seeing similarities between things that at first seem very different.

From Teaching Global Literacy Using Mnemonics by Joan Ebbesmeyer.
Westport, CT: Libraries Unlimited/Teacher Ideas Press. Copyright © 2006.

South America Activities: Magical Metaphors

Activity 2. Research and work in pairs to find words that describe both of the following pairs.

1. The rain forest and a labyrinth

Can get lost in both of them		

2. A piranha and a nightmare

3. Trees and cathedrals

Both are tall and majestic		

4. A jaguar and a king

Both are powerful		

5. The forest floor and a dungeon

Frightening at times		

6. A tapir and illusion

7. A chameleon and an actor

Both change often		

8. Jungle mushrooms and nightlights

From *Teaching Global Literacy Using Mnemonics* by Joan Ebbesmeyer.
Westport, CT: Libraries Unlimited/Teacher Ideas Press. Copyright © 2006.

South America Activities: Magical Metaphors

Activity 3. You are learning to write using metaphors. It is a creative way of writing. Write a paragraph on South America using metaphors.

Example

South America is the land of the towering Andes Mountains, dense tropical rain forests, and great open plains of grass and scrub. The mountains are great stone treasure chests filled with silver, tin, and other valuable minerals. They stretch the entire length of the continent on the western side, from Columbia in the north through Argentina in the south.

The rain forests of the northeastern area are the largest in the world. The Amazon rain forest is a labyrinth of trees, plants, and dense foliage. It is a moist oven where heat and humidity have made the forest what it is! The forest is a life-giver, helping to supply Earth with its needed nutrients, found in the magnificent trees, standing like cathedrals reaching for the heavens above. It is a pharmacy containing plants that hold the secret to healing. It is a survivor, trying to save its jungle trees and plants as they are being destroyed by people filled with greed and seeking power.

The Amazon River is a highway of water that covers the width of the great continent from Columbia through Brazil, finally empting into the Atlantic Ocean.

- Can you find the metaphors in the description above? Underline them.

- What metaphors could you use for the Atacoma Desert, Angel Falls, or the many unique animals of South America? Write any you think of in the spaces below. Try to see and think of things in different ways. You might see a snake as a deadly ribbon, an armadillo as an armored tank, a piranha as a man-eating nightmare, and the jaguar as a jungle king.

Metaphoric thinking will help make your writing more interesting, creative, and flexible. It will help you see things in new ways—from a different perspective. Choose a person, country, animal, or thing that is associated with South America and write as many metaphors as you can think of to describe it. Think how creative your descriptive paragraph will be! And imagine the different insights you will gain by thinking of South America in metaphor.

_____
_____
_____
_____
_____
_____
_____
_____
_____
_____
_____
_____

From *Teaching Global Literacy Using Mnemonics* by Joan Ebbesmeyer.
Westport, CT: Libraries Unlimited/Teacher Ideas Press. Copyright © 2006.

South America Activities: Imagination

The Most Important Tool of Human Intelligence (Standards 4, 17, and 18)

Teach your students that with imagination, we can bring the past back to life, form mental images, look into the future, and invent new realities. It is as important in teaching geography as it is in any other part of the curriculum.

Although we cannot literally transport our students to the far reaches of the world, we can help our students to form mental pictures of these places through our descriptive words and stories. We can help them travel in time back to life in the past and forward to the possibilities of the future; we can help them understand the important characters and cultures of places such as the countries of South America through the use of *imagination*.

Speaking and storytelling of the mighty Amazon River that rises in the Andes and flows almost four thousand miles to the Atlantic Ocean is exciting when students learn that it is large enough in some places to accommodate ocean liners.

The Andes, covering the entire western coast of the continent, are not only the world's longest mountain range, but they also hold many secrets such as the ancient Inca city of Machu Picchu.

1. Ask students to imagine and draw the ancient Incan fortress city of Machu Picchu, built on a five-square-mile series of terraces carved on a mountain that was more than eight thousand feet high.

    If they can't imagine how this could look, find pictures on the Web sites of ancient civilizations. Thousands of people still visit the once proud city of the ancient Inca Empire.

2. Have students try to imagine a mountain range that stretches 4,500 miles long. This is longer than the entire width of the United States. The Andes are found along the entire western coast of South America. They are high mountains, reaching 22,000 feet. They are also very beautiful and hold valuable minerals.

South America Activities: Use Your Imagination

Look at the outline of South America below. Label the countries that contain the Andean Mountain range.

Outline of South America. Now you are familiar with the thirteen land regions of South America. Can you label the countries on the map above?

From *Teaching Global Literacy Using Mnemonics* by Joan Ebbesmeyer.
Westport, CT: Libraries Unlimited/Teacher Ideas Press. Copyright © 2006.

Chapter 5

Europe

Europe

Many Americans can trace their ancestry back to the European countries. There is a strong tie between the cultures, ideology, governments, and civilizations of Europe and North America, two continents separated by the Atlantic Ocean.

It started in the 1500s when English, Dutch, Spanish, and French explorers arrived at the eastern and southern parts of America. It continued after the Industrial Revolution, when thousands of poor people left Europe to search for a new and better life in the United States.

After thousands of years of farming and many years of industrialization, Europe has changed in its landscape, and because of the great cities that have grown up in the many different countries, there is not much wilderness left on the continent.

Europe has many different peoples, languages, and cultures, but the European Union and a single currency (the euro) are helping to create an economic and political unity among the many countries.

Suggested Reading

Picture Books

Oberman, Sheldon. *By the Hanukkah Light.* Illustrated by Neil Waldman. Boyds Mills Press, 1997.

> Hanukkah is the Jewish celebration of lights, and this story tells of one year's festival when Grandpa shares his memories of this celebration during the Hitler years in Germany. The story is sad, telling of the six million Jews who died during the Holocaust, but happy as one learns that courage and goodness can triumph over evil.

Redmond, Shirley Raye. *Pigeon Hero.* Illustrated by Doris Ettlinger. Aladdin Library, 2003.

> This is a Ready-to-Read book that will appeal to beginning readers. It tells an exciting story, based on fact, about how a town in Italy was saved from destruction through the efforts of an astounding carrier pigeon named G.I. Joe. The pigeon faced many dangers in accomplishing his amazing flight but was rewarded as no other pigeon had ever been rewarded before.

Tryszynska-Frederick, Luba, as told to Michelle Me Dann. *Luba—The Angel of Bergen Belsen.* Illustrated by Ann Marshall. Tricycle Press, 2003.

> Luba is another true story that should be of great interest to elementary and secondary school readers. The story tells of fifty-four children left to die in the bitter cold by the Nazis during World War II. They were found, still alive, behind the infamous Bergen-Belsen concentration camp by Luba Tryszynska. She was also a prisoner of the Germans.
>
> The dangers and sacrifices that Luba faced to save these children will evoke deep emotion in the reader and bring an understanding of why she is called the Angel of Bergen-Belsen!

Chapter Books

Lowry, Lois. *Number the Stars.* Houghton Mifflin, 1989.

> Annamarie Johansen lives in German-occupied Denmark during World War II. Life is not easy with Nazi soldiers watching their every move. There are food shortages, rationing, and the knowledge that their beloved king has lost his power to rule the country.

However, the ten-year-old Annamarie can bear everything except knowing her best friend, Ellen, is in mortal danger because she is a Jew. The Johansens prepare a desperate plan to save Ellen and her family. Annamarie is determined to be a part of the plan.

Garrigue, Sheila. *All The Children Were Sent Away.* Bradbury Press, 1976.

It's hard to imagine the terror and sadness of being torn away from your home, your country, and your parents at the tender age of eight. Sara Warren and thousands of other children had to suffer this fear and separation to survive the German bombing and occupation of European countries during the 1940s.

Sara is sent from bomb-weary England to the safety of Canada in North America. There are many adventures on the ship that carries her across the ocean. Some are pleasant, like making friends with Maggie and Ernie. But the appearance of a German submarine is an experience that everyone feared.

Morpurgo, Michael. *Waiting for Anya.* Viking Penguin 1997.

Millions of helpless civilians had to undergo danger and deprivation to survive in Nazi Europe during World War II. If you were a Jew, the danger was critical. Hitler wanted *all* Jews killed—every man, woman, and child.

In this story, Jo and Benjamin decide they have to save as many people as they can, even though it could lead to their own death.

As the German soldiers march victoriously into their French town, the two begin the precarious trip to safety in the hills. It takes a great deal of luck and courage to be successful.

The Shadow
A Mnemonic Story about Europe

Shadows can have very interesting or very dull experiences as they go through life. The excitement depends on the person they are shadowing! The shadow I want to tell you about had some unbelievable journeys across a continent called Europe. By the time you follow this shadow and his human connection, you will know all forty-three countries of Europe and much of what happened there more than sixty years ago.

It all started with a leader who wanted to rule the world! He already controlled the country of Germany, but he was greedy and decided he could conquer the whole continent of Europe—and perhaps the whole world! His name was Adolf Hitler. And the shadow in our story was Hitler's.

Germany is situated in the middle of the northern part of Europe. Hitler marched his powerful army to the east and conquered **Poland** and Czechoslovakia (now the **Czech Republic** and **Slovakia**). The shadow went along. Hitler was so pleased with what happened in the east that he decided to go west next time. He swept through the windmill country of the **Netherlands,** then down to **Belgium, Liechtenstein,** and **Luxembourg.** The biggest prize yet now lay within his grasp, and he captured **France** in all her glory. The shadow couldn't believe how quickly and ruthlessly the armies overran the countries. It was called a blitzkrieg—a lightning strike—because that's what it felt like, a swift bolt of lightning. The people and their armies were conquered before they realized what was happening.

Next Hitler took over **Denmark,** the small country just above Germany; then he sailed across the North Sea to the three finger-like countries of **Norway, Sweden,** and **Finland.** The shadow understood why Sweden remained neutral in this war, and why Finland joined Germany to fight against all the other countries. They did so out of fear! It seemed that nothing could stop this man who was determined to rule the world. The shadow believed he was connected to the most powerful man in the whole world—the most powerful leader in history. Where would Hitler strike next?

The shadow soon found out! After conquering so many countries of Europe, Hitler was "**Hungary**" for **Turkey** fried in **Greece** and served with an alphabet soup of countries, all ending with the letter *A*. The soup consisted of **Albania, Bulgaria, Macedonia,** and **Romania.** Now his armies were marching south.

Hitler defeated most of the land area of Europe. The remaining countries and their people wondered what they could do to save themselves from being overtaken by this monster.

Some followed the example of Finland and joined Hitler's cause. One of these countries was **Italy,** the country shaped like a boot. The boot has two tiny countries inside of it. They are **San Marino** near the eastern coast and **Vatican City,** in the west, surrounded by the ancient city of Rome. Vatican City is the smallest country in the world. Italy looks as if it will step on the little country of **Malta** below it. The two countries above Italy differed in their actions. **Switzerland** became a neutral country and fought no one, while **Austria** was conquered.

And there was **Spain** in the lower part of Europe. Spain with its "front porch," **Portugal,** and its "back door," **Andorra,** make up the Iberian peninsula. Spain remained neutral, but friendly, to Hitler. The shadow felt very smug about the whole situation. Surely the few countries still unconquered would fold like a weak fan before the might of the Nazi forces and their allies. What a life he could look forward to as all peoples bowed before him and the human to whom he was connected!

From *Teaching Global Literacy Using Mnemonics* by Joan Ebbesmeyer.
Westport, CT: Libraries Unlimited/Teacher Ideas Press. Copyright © 2006.

He looked forward to the next campaign and wondered what new conquests might be made now that Japan had joined their side against the United States of America and its allies, Russia and the United Kingdom. These countries needed help. Hitler's army had invaded Russia and was terrorizing the United Kingdom with a brutal bombing campaign. Did the Americans think they could change the course of the war? Didn't they realize that the Axis forces of Germany and Japan were invincible, Hitler and the shadow wondered?

The shadow knew that Hitler would seize total control of the continent with a successful invasion of the last two countries. The great island country, **United Kingdom,** across the North Sea to the east of Germany and the Union of Soviet Socialist Republic (USSR; also often called **Russia**) that lay to the north and west would *not* give up and surrender. Today the USSR is called the Russian Federation; the USSR no longer exists.

The shadow realized the people who made up the United Kingdom were from the countries of England, Scotland, Wales, and Northern Ireland. They were very courageous, but the shadow watched as Hitler sent his bombers over night and day to destroy their countries and strike fear in the people's hearts. However, these people had a brave king and queen who refused to leave their people to seek safety. Instead, they stayed in the capital city of London where the bombing was the worst. They inspired the people with their courage and waited for the Americans to come to their aid. In addition, the British had a unique leader, Prime Minister Winston Churchill, who convinced the people that they would fight in the buildings, they would fight in the streets, they would fight in their homes, but they would never, ever, surrender!

Ireland, which borders Northern Ireland, remained neutral, and the arctic country of **Iceland** was of no value to Hitler.

Russia was invaded, but not defeated, and the shadow had his first misgivings when this vast land was invaded. Did Hitler realize how immense and unforgiving this gigantic country was? Did Hitler remember the terrible Russian winters and the many other invaders, such as Napoleon, who were defeated by the unrelenting cold and the steadfast courage of the Russian people? The shadow cringed when he heard of the defeat on the eastern front. He shrank from the truth of the hundreds of thousands of German soldiers who were killed and captured by the Russians. He shivered and shook knowing that the Allies—the United States, Britain, and USSR—would destroy him and his human connection. In truth, though, he knew they had destroyed themselves!

And in fact, that's what happened: Hitler destroyed himself, and the shadow was gone forever. After the Allies invaded Normandy in France, the USSR defeated Germany. Europe finally found peace again, and across the continent there was more light than shadow!

Many years later, at the end of the twentieth century, some European countries changed dramatically. Their names changed, too. The USSR became known as Russia (or the Russian Federation). Some land on the western side of Russia broke away and formed new countries.

We could say that:

Each Little Land By USSR Moved!

E for **Estonia**

L for **Latvia**

L for **Lithuania**

B for **Belarus**

U for **Ukraine**

M for **Moldavia**

From *Teaching Global Literacy Using Mnemonics* by Joan Ebbesmeyer.
Westport, CT: Libraries Unlimited/Teacher Ideas Press. Copyright © 2006.

Another country, Yugoslavia, divided itself around the same time and became:

S. C. B. S.
Several Countries Border Serbia & Montenegro

S for **Slovenia**

C for **Croatia**

B for **Bosnia/Herzegovina**

S for **Serbia/Montenegro**

Europe became the continent of the forty-three countries, some new and some that we know from our journey with the dark shadow of Hitler. Here are the forty-three countries:

1. GERMANY	11. SWEDEN	21. ITALY	31. IRELAND
2. POLAND	12. FINLAND	22. SAN MARINO	32. ICELAND
3. CZECH REPUBLIC	13. HUNGARY	23. VATICAN CITY	33. RUSSIA
4. SLOVAKIA	14. TURKEY	24. MALTA	34. ESTONIA
5. NETHERLANDS	15. GREECE	25. SWITZERLAND	35. LATVIA
6. BELGIUM	16. ALBANIA	26. AUSTRIA	36. LITHUANIA
7. LIECHTENSTEIN	17. BULGARIA	27. SPAIN	37. BELARUS
8. FRANCE	18. MACEDONIA	28. PORTUGAL	38. UKRAINE
9. DENMARK	19. ROMANIA	29. ANDORRA	39. MOLDAVIA
10. NORWAY	20. SERBIA/ MONTENEGRO	30. UNITED KINGDOM	40. SLOVENIA
41. CROATIA	42. BOSNIA/ HERZEGOVINA	43. LUXEMBOURG	

Europe Activities: Using the Atlas and Learning to Mind Map

Mind Mapping—Countries and Rivers (Standards 1–4)

Activity 1. Listen to the mnemonic story of "The Shadow" again. Using a magic marker and a map of Europe, trace the journey he makes, starting at Germany, to many of the countries of Europe as you hear the story unfold. If you get confused, raise your hand, and the reader will stop until you have found your location. You may want to work in pairs.

Activity 2. Now that you are more familiar with the locations of the various countries, take a map of Europe that has all the countries outlined, but not labeled. Work in small groups to locate and label each country by memory. Keep the story available if you get confused.

From *Teaching Global Literacy Using Mnemonics* by Joan Ebbesmeyer.
Westport, CT: Libraries Unlimited/Teacher Ideas Press. Copyright © 2006.

Europe Activities: Researching the Rivers of Europe (Standards 7, 11, and 15)

The many rivers of Europe provide water for irrigation and power to generate electricity. They also serve as major transportation routes for industry and pleasure. Now that you know the countries and location of Europe, work in pairs to see if you can connect the important European rivers with the country of their source. Use your atlas and draw the rivers' courses on your maps. Add other rivers you discover.

Volga	Germany
Danube	Poland
Tiber	Spain
Seine	Russia
Tagus	Italy
Rhine	United Kingdom
Elbe	Germany
Po	Czech Republic
Thames	France
Oder	Italy

From *Teaching Global Literacy Using Mnemonics* by Joan Ebbesmeyer.
Westport, CT: Libraries Unlimited/Teacher Ideas Press. Copyright © 2006.

Europe Activities: Physical Features—Webbing (Standards 7, 9–12)

As you learn about the rivers of Europe, you will web naturally into many connections. A good way to illustrate the expansions of learning would be creating a web on a tag board drawing like the one below.

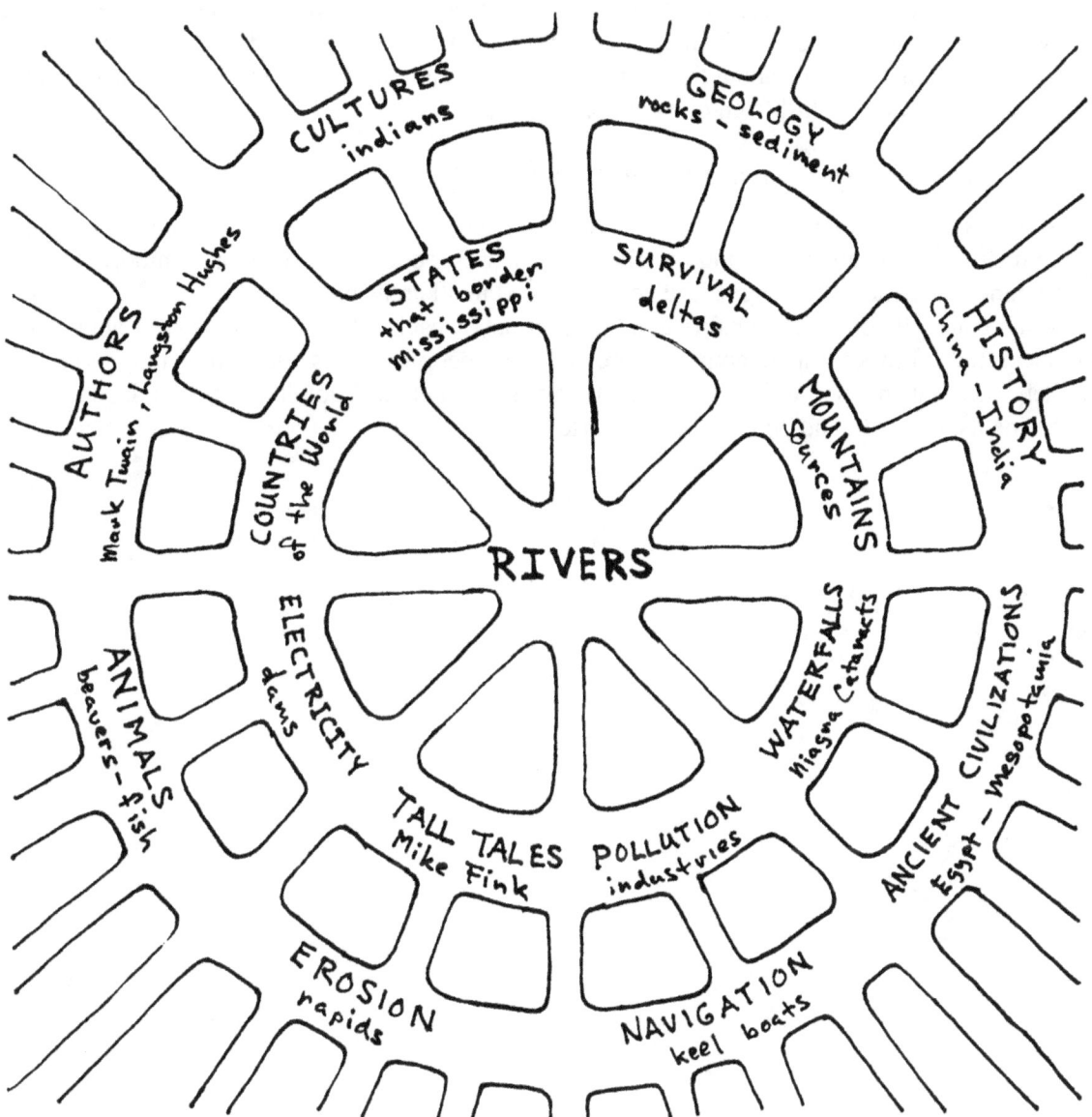

Add as many associations as you can to the web of rivers. It will help you understand the connection between all things and the physical processes that shape the patterns of Earth's surface, as well as the processes of human settlement.

From *Teaching Global Literacy Using Mnemonics* by Joan Ebbesmeyer.
Westport, CT: Libraries Unlimited/Teacher Ideas Press. Copyright © 2006.

Europe Activities: Critical Thinking

Questioning and Transfer (Standards 13–15, 17, and 18)

The mnemonic story "The Shadow" will aid students' understanding of World War II and post-war Europe. The fall of Hitler's Germany, the Allies' help in reconstruction, and then the Cold War dramatically changed the continent. Students can be led into an understanding of how the forces of conflict influenced the division and control of Earth's surface, how human actions change the physical environment, and how geography helps to determine the present, past, and future of a continent.

Understanding can come about through the use of Socratic questioning techniques and by learning to transfer a thinking skill from one context to another.

Example—Transfer: Compare and Contrast (Upper Grades)

Students learn to compare and contrast at an early age. Use this skill in geography by comparing and contrasting the locations, mountains, rivers, industries, people, language, and important leaders of the countries of Europe. This method could be used in all areas of the world.

A sentence with one commonality and one contrast on each subject would be sufficient. See the worksheet that follows for an example. There are many people, places, and things that could be researched using this method to interest students in expanding their knowledge and understanding of the continents, cultures, and peoples of the world.

Europe Activities: Critical Thinking

Questioning and Transfer

Show what you have learned about the people, rivers, countries, and cultures of Europe by using comparison (same) and contrasting (different) sentences to show your knowledge.

Write a sentence showing an important commonality and a significant contrast on the following connections to Europe. What is the same and what is different about the two things?

1. Iceland and Italy

   _____
   _____
   _____

2. The Volga River and the Danube River

   _____
   _____
   _____

3. Adolf Hitler and Winston Churchill

   _____
   _____
   _____

4. The Alps Mountains and the Apennines Mountains

   The Alps and the Apennines are both great mountains in Europe, but the Alps are located north of Italy in Germany, and the Apennines stretch down the length of the country of Italy.

5. The language of Great Britain and that of Macedonia

   _____
   _____
   _____

6. The financial stability of Sweden and the situation in Armenia

   _____
   _____
   _____

7. The industrial development of Germany and that of Albania

   _____
   _____
   _____

From *Teaching Global Literacy Using Mnemonics* by Joan Ebbesmeyer.
Westport, CT: Libraries Unlimited/Teacher Ideas Press. Copyright © 2006.

Socratic Questioning

Questioning is used to assess comprehension, to guide and develop student thinking, and to stimulate an understanding of connections. Teachers serve as models in their skillful use of questioning, thus leading to students' ability to ask divergent and open-ended questions of their own.

Teachers need to develop critical thinking by asking *fewer* questions about who, what, where, and when, and *more* open-ended questions that lead to prediction, analysis, differentiation, and connections.

Examples

1. *Lower level students:* Give an example of two large rivers of Europe and why they are important.

   Upper level students: Give an example of what thousands of years of farming and hundreds of years of industrialization have done to the landscape of Europe.

2. *Lower level students:* What countries make up Scandinavia?

   Upper level students: What do I mean when I say the Vikings, with their discoveries of new lands and their fearsome raids along the coasts of Europe, changed the continent forever?

3. *Lower level students:* Can you give me evidence to support the fact that the British Isles have a moderate climate, even though they are located in northern Europe?

   Upper level students: Can you give me evidence to support the critical importance of the Marshall Plan to the European countries after World War II?

4. *Lower level students:* How are the countries of San Marino and Vatican City connected to Italy?

   Upper level students: How does the formation of the European Union (EU) apply to the increase of economic and political unity of the continent?

5. *Lower level students:* What do you think about the fact that many animals were destroyed to make way for the big cities and factories of Europe?

   Upper level students: What do you think is important about Northern Ireland remaining a part of the United Kingdom rather than returning to the Republic of Ireland?

Europe Activities: Assessment

(Standards 2, 4, 7, 13)

Assessment 1. This type of questioning should lead students into a deeper understanding of and new insights into all things connected to Europe. Once they become familiar with more open-ended questions and find more creative ways to reach deeper understanding, they work in groups to learn about European countries and create their own questions to compete and assess the knowledge of other groups.

Example: The Five-Clue Game

In five-clue games, students are given five clues to guess an answer. Five points are earned for the first and most difficult clue; four for the second, less difficult clue; and so on. Student groups create their own quiz questions.

1. I am a central European country.
2. I maintain no regular armed forces for defense.
3. My capital city is Bern.
4. I am located between France and Austria.
5. I am a beautiful Alpine country, known for my watches.

Answer: Switzerland

1. I stretch over two continents.
2. I have the longest river in Europe.
3. You'll find part of the Trans-Siberian railway here.
4. I am the largest country in Europe.
5. My capital city is Moscow.

Answer: Russia

1. I am a southern European country.
2. I am a peninsula.
3. My origin is told in the myth of Romulus and Remus.
4. Gladiators once fought in my ancient coliseum.
5. My capital is the home of a great ancient empire.

Answer: Italy

1. I am a body of water bordering Europe.
2. A large ridge runs north and south through my center.
3. I touch Europe on my east and North America on my west.
4. Romans named me after the Atlas Mountains in Africa.
5. I am the second largest ocean.

Answer: Atlantic Ocean

1. I am a western European country.
2. I am named for a German tribe that invaded me in the third century.
3. I am the largest country bordering Italy.
4. Monaco is a very small country inside of me.
5. Paris is the name of my capital city.

Answer: France

1. I am a country, found in the far north of Europe.
2. I am also an island in the Atlantic Ocean.
3. I have daylight for twenty-four hours during the month of June.
4. My capital city is Reykjavik.
5. My name comes from being so "icy."

Answer: Iceland

1. I am found on the British Isles.
2. One third of the food we eat must be imported.
3. Industry is important—it pays for imported food.
4. I'm actually a union made up of four countries.
5. London is my capital city.

Answer: United Kingdom

1. I am a body of water.
2. I connect the Atlantic Ocean and the North Sea.
3. I lie between England and France.
4. I am the world's busiest sea passage.
5. An American was the first woman to swim across it.

Answer: English Channel

1. I am one of the "low countries."
2. Almost a quarter of my land has been reclaimed from the sea.
3. Anne Frank wrote her famous World War II diary here.
4. People call me the "windmill country."
5. Amsterdam is the name of my capital city.

Answer: The Netherlands

Students should be encouraged to create their own clue questions for competition in their classroom and between other classes. The best way to learn is to teach!

Assessment 2. Another fun type of assessment can be done using four-line rhymes that students create for their classmates. They could draw maps of each one, illustrate them, and make a book for the school library.

Examples

Who Am I?

I am the smallest country

You will ever see,

And I can be found

In the middle of Italy.

Answer: Vatican City

I have four areas in one.

They call me UK.

I'm northeast of Ireland.

Now, what do you say?

Answer: United Kingdom

Iberian Peninsula

That's what they call me.

But I'm more than one country.

Can you name all three?

Answer: Spain, Portugal, Andorra

What Am I?

Across southern Europe

I'm a mountain range, grand,

From Spain to Caspian Sea

I cover the land.

Answer: Alps Mountains

The longest river

In Europe you'll see.

It flows through Russia.

The name starts with a V.

Answer: Volga River

It's a university

Its name begins with an "O."

A famous school in England

That helps good minds to grow.

Answer: Oxford University

Chapter 6
Africa

Africa

Africa is the second largest continent in the world, and this vast land contains a mixture of many, many ethnic groups, cultures, land regions, and languages. The world is intrigued by Earth's largest desert, the Sahara, in the north; the great savanna grasslands; and tropical rain forests of central Africa with its wild, roaming animals. Africa also has the beautiful modern cities of Cape Town and Johannesburg in the south.

Africa is a world of multiformity—on one hand, one finds poverty, civil wars, political instability, the spread of AIDS, drought, and illiteracy. On the other hand, it is a land of great potential wealth, with modern cities and unbelievable scenic beauty, with its magnificent waterfalls, snow-capped mountains, clear blue lakes, and wide rivers. The main rivers are the Nile, Congo, and Niger. Kilimanjaro is the highest mountain peak in Africa. The main groups of people are the Arab and Berber peoples living north of the Sahara, and the black Africans (more than one thousand ethnic groups) who live south of the desert.

Suggested Reading

Picture Books (Grade 1–3)

Geraghty, Paul. *The Hunter.* Crown Publishers, 1994.

    Jamina finds adventure when she goes with Grandfather to collect honey in the bush country of Africa. She is most interested in finding an elephant and succeeds in her quest when she wanders away and becomes lost in the bush.

    The baby elephant that Jamina finds has lost his mother to the hunters and will surely die unless Jamina can find a way to reach the elephant herd. She remembers the advice Grandfather gave her for times of danger. She follows the wise words and manages to save the elephant and herself.

Greenfield, Eloise. *Africa Dream.* Illustrated by Carole Byard. HarperTrophy, 1997.

    This is a great book for all children, but especially those of African descent. For African American children, the words and pictures will provoke pride in learning about their past and instill a sense of belonging to an international world family.

MacDonald, Suse. *Nanta's Lion.* Morrow Junior Books, 1995.

    This book is a search-and-find adventure that may appeal to young children. It is filled with pages shaped to the grasslands and mountains of the African Maasai village where little Nanta lives.

    Nanta proves to be a curious and brave girl as she listens to the hunters prepare for a lion hunt and then decides to find a lion for herself. Her journey allows her to see many wild animals, but only the book's reader is allowed to see the lion!

Weir, Bob, and Wendy Weir. *Panther Dream. A Story of the African Rainforest.* Hyperion Books for Children, 1991.

    Lokuli is a lad of Africa who lives in the rain forest. His life includes wild animals, Pygmies, forest spirits, and equatorial heat and humidity. As in most cultures, Lokuli's life is influenced by the myths and stories handed down from his ancestors.

    When Lokuli's tribe has difficulty in finding enough meat to eat, the boy listens to the story of the panther and how he stores his food high in a tree. Lokuli borrows a spear and enters the jungle to find the panther's food. He finds a monkey, a hawk, and a black and white hornbill;

then he falls asleep beneath a large tree. The panther awakens him and tells him to take only the food he needs and not to abuse the land or the animals. Lokuli promises to obey these words.

In reward the panther shows him where to find food for the tribe and makes Lokuli a hero. A new African myth is created!

Chapter Books

Clayton, Bess. *Story for a Black Night*. Parnassus Press, 1982.

Story for a Black Night is a book that brings you close to long-ago Africa and its people. Momo, who is the father, tells the story of a time when he was a very young boy. It is a tale of good and evil, of sickness and death, and a struggle between the life and death spirits. More important, it is a story of a mother's love and suffering and of a family's ability to endure.

Farmer, Nancy. *A Girl Named Disaster*. Orchard Books, 1996.

This book gives a clear picture of the Africans' belief in the spirit world. Nhamo undertakes a long and dangerous journey down the waterways of southern Africa. It is the only way to escape from a marriage that is being forced upon the twelve-year-old girl. She comes close to drowning, starving, and being killed by a group of wild baboons.

Nhamo faces many daily terrors and dark, frightening nights, but she has courage and the spirits of her mother and grandmother to sustain her.

Hansen, Joyce. *The Captive*. Scholastic, 1994.

An African boy, Kofi, is a member of the Ashanti tribe that lives in the western region of the continent. His father is the Great Chief. He has several wives and many children. Their lives follow a happy pattern of work, village life, and family, until the evil of slavery is visited upon them.

Kofi cannot believe his own people worked with the white slavers, capturing young boys and sailing the ocean to sell them to Puritan farmers in New England.

How Kofi survives in the new world, eventually finds freedom, and then returns to his home in Africa makes a dramatic and interesting story.

Jacobs, Shannon K. *Song of the Giraffe*. Little, Brown & Company, 1991.

Kisana was a small, light-skinned girl in an African tribe of tall, dark natives. She grows up feeling "different" and of little worth. However, she is brave and kind to the wild animals of the nearby jungle. This kindness is rewarded with a dream from the spirit world. The dream message from the graceful giraffe leads the way to finding water for the desperate village. Kisana will never lack a feeling of self-worth or respect from the villagers from that day on!

Reeves, Nicholas, with Nan Froman. *Into the Mummy's Tomb*. Scholastic/Madison Press Book, 1992.

Of all the ancient Pharaoh's tombs uncovered in Egypt, the most exciting and valuable find was that of Tutankhamen (King Tut). In this book, you can read about the hidden steps leading into the mountain and the awesome treasure that was buried with the boy king.

The illustrations show clearly how Tut was prepared for his journey into the afterlife. His mummy and all the treasures of the tomb were found intact. These artifacts are of immeasurable value, and the things such as his chariot, a boat, toys, statues, and furniture provide vivid insight into the culture of Egypt three thousand years ago. The secrets of the ancient Egyptians' beliefs on religion, death, and the afterlife are revealed.

Mubatu Discovers the World Called Africa
A Mnemonic Story about Africa

Mubatu was a boy who belonged to the Tuareg people (who are nomads, or members of a wandering tribe) of Africa. He lived in the largest desert in the world, the Sahara, and thought that all of Africa must be desert land, just like his part of the continent. One day when he was helping his grandfather herd the camels, he mentioned this to him. Grandfather laughed and then began to teach and tell about the Africa Mubatu knew so little.

Grandfather took a stick and drew an outline of the large continent in the dust. Mubatu thought the drawing looked like the head and neck of an animal that was facing west. The animal had a horn at the back.

Grandfather told him the Sahara Desert covered only one-third of the continent, but it was large enough to include thirteen countries. When Mubatu asked their names, Grandfather told him to think of the humming sound of the desert. Mubatu began to hum with the sound of the "M," and Grandfather began at the top to section off the northwestern part of his dust map and to outline the "M" countries, **Morocco, Mauritania,** and **Mali.** He told Mubatu to imagine the sweep of the sand blowing over *An* awesome **Algeria, and** Tiny **Tunisia,** Linking **Libya** to ancient **Egypt.** Mubatu saw the outlines of these countries that stretched west to east ending at the Red Sea.

Grandfather took his stick back to the western side and to the M countries. He said that N came after M, so the next country was **Niger** bumping into Cheerful **chad** riding in his **"Sudan"!** Mubatu laughed at the play on words.

Then Grandfather looked very sad as he spoke about the last four countries of the Sahara. He told Mubatu these were part of the Horn of Africa countries—because the area resembled a horn. The Horn is one of the poorest regions on Earth. The droughts (very dry weather) had killed the growing **Seed,** and thousands of their people there had died of hunger.

Mubatu thought about the word *s-e-e-d* to remember the countries:

Somalia, Ethiopia, Eritrea, Djibouti (Jaboote).

"These are the countries of northern Africa," said Grandfather, "just hum and then connect letters and words to help you remember the names.

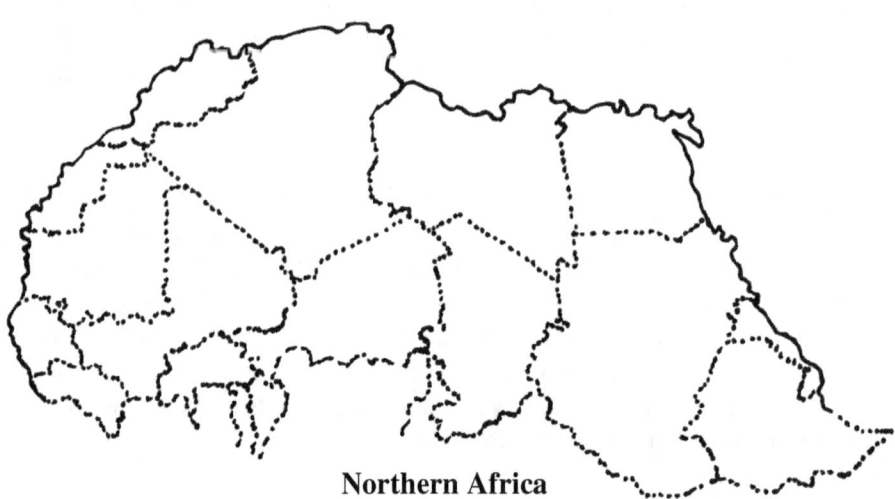

Northern Africa

From *Teaching Global Literacy Using Mnemonics* by Joan Ebbesmeyer.
Westport, CT: Libraries Unlimited/Teacher Ideas Press. Copyright © 2006.

"Now," said Grandfather, "On to the countries of the equator, below the Sahara, where we'll visit the sub-Saharan grasslands and make more connections!" Mubatu couldn't believe all the countries Grandfather outlined below the Sahara. It looked like a patchwork quilt, with the equator dividing the continent into two large pieces. He wondered how he could possibly learn the names of all these nations.

Again, Grandfather started on the western side and made fifteen small Circles to show the islands of **Cape Verde,** which lay directly off the African coast, and the Snake country, **Senegal.** Senegal had wrapped itself around the first of the six G countries. **Gambia** was in the snake's mouth, and below it was **Guinea Bissau, Guinea, Ghana, Equatorial Guinea,** and **Gabon.** Mubatu wondered whether all the countries' names began with G, but Grandfather showed him there were two **L** countries called **Liberia** and **Sierra Leone,** the elephant nation, **Cote d'Ivoire,** and three more that Grandfather connected to Mubatu's dog Togo. They are called **Togo, Benin,** and **Burkino Faso.** "Connect **Nigeria** to Niger directly above it," said Grandfather, "and you have arrived at the equator and the central part of Africa. Before we leave the equator, please remember the tiny island, **Sao Tome and Principe**" (pronounced San-Toe-May and Principe). Can you imagine living on the equator?

Mubatu was excited because he knew they were in the tropical rain forest area and in the safari country where many wild animals roamed the grasslands. Also nearby were the countries that surrounded the source of the great Nile River.

Sure enough, Grandfather said to think "**C**" and **Central** to remember **Central African Republic, Cameroon, and Congo.** Think "safari" to remember **Kenya** and **Tanzania.** Think Nile River to remember **Uganda, Rwanda, and Burundi**—the countries that surround the source of the river Nile, as it starts its journey, flowing not south as most rivers do, but *north* to the Mediterranean Sea.

How diverse this great continent of fifty-three countries is! We have traveled mentally from Morocco, across the largest desert in the world, Sahara, to the pyramids of Egypt. We have crossed the equator, seen the tropical rain forest and the Great Rift Valley that extends for more than three thousand miles down the eastern side of the continent. We imagine the three great lakes that are the source of the longest river in the world, the Nile, which runs *north* for more than four thousand miles to the immense delta in Egypt and then empties into the Mediterranean Sea.

Central Africa

From *Teaching Global Literacy Using Mnemonics* by Joan Ebbesmeyer.
Westport, CT: Libraries Unlimited/Teacher Ideas Press. Copyright © 2006.

Mubatu was anxious to learn what connections they would use to remember the names of the southern African countries. However, Grandfather said it would be very similar to the connections of the north, only this time they would start on the eastern side. So, Mubatu began to hum the sound of the "M" as Grandfather outlined the large island of **Madagascar,** directly to the east of the coastal nations of **Mozambique** and **Malawi.**

Then to the western side, we begin with A–B - to Z. **A for Angola, B for Botswana** to **Z for Zambia** and **Zimbabwe.** When we connect the very dry deserts of the south, we think of the Kalahari and Namib Deserts found in the country of **Namibia,** which borders the southernmost country of Africa, which, of course, is called **South Africa.** South Africa and Italy have something in common: they both have two countries within their boundaries. In Italy they are San Marino and Vatican City. In South Africa, they are **Lesotho** and **Swaziland.**

Mubatu decided they must have covered all the countries, but Grandfather insisted there were three remaining island countries surrounding Madagascar. "So Many Countries!" cried Mubatu. Grandfather laughed and told Mubatu that he had made the last connection. **S for Seychelles** (say-shells), **M for Mauritius,** and **C for Comoros.**

Southern Africa

When Mubatu and Grandfather had identified the fifty-three countries of Africa, they walked away from the drawing in the dust, filled with the thoughts of their vast continent, the millions of people from many different cultures, and the hundreds of different languages they spoke. Mubatu was sad to think of the many civil wars and famine that afflicted the people, but he was proud of the progress many nations had made since they fought and finally received their independence from the European countries in the twentieth century.

They had traveled in imagination from the Atlas Mountains in the north to the Drakenberg Mountains in the south. They had gone from the old, old city of Timbuktu in the west to the eastern ancient cultures of Egypt and Ethiopia. They had imagined the elephants, rhinoceroses, zebras, and lions living in the savanna grasslands. They had witnessed Mount Kilimanjaro, the highest point in Africa, and watched in awe one of the world's largest waterfalls, Victoria Falls.

Mubatu had learned much about the wonderful and unique continent of Africa. It was enough to wonder about for the rest of his life!!

From *Teaching Global Literacy Using Mnemonics* by Joan Ebbesmeyer.
Westport, CT: Libraries Unlimited/Teacher Ideas Press. Copyright © 2006.

Africa Activities

Understanding the Physical and Human Characteristics of Sahara (Standards 4, 7–9)

The Sahara is the largest desert in the world and covers nearly one-third of the vast continent of Africa. Many people in the Saharan countries live a hard life as they try to survive by growing their crops while the desert is spreading and destroying farmland. This causes famine, and water becomes a precious commodity to many of the thirteen countries of the northern desert.

In the activities that follow, "Where There Is Water, There Is Life!" is for lower grade levels; "What's the Problem???" is for middle grades, and "Waste Not, Want Not" is for upper grade levels.

Where There Is Water, There Is Life!: Recall

We are fortunate that the resource of life-giving water is renewable. Look at the drawing below and label the three processes of the water cycle that constantly provide Earth with water.

Which one is water turning into vapor? (It's called evaporation.)

Which one is water vapor turning into droplets? (It's called condensation.)

Which process is water falling back to Earth as rain? (It's called precipitation.)

Label the illustration with 1, 2, and 3 as follows: 1. condensation, 2. evaporation, and 3. precipitation.

From *Teaching Global Literacy Using Mnemonics* by Joan Ebbesmeyer.
Westport, CT: Libraries Unlimited/Teacher Ideas Press. Copyright © 2006.

Africa Activities: What's the Problem???

Problem Solving

Water is renewable—but precious! Without it, there can be no life on Earth. It is used so often in our daily lives that we begin to take it for granted. We need to realize how useful it is in our lives and how to conserve it rather than waste it. By understanding how vital water is, we can begin to understand the problems of drought-ridden countries.

Work in groups and list as many uses of water in your daily life as you can.

What was the most unusual use you thought of? _____
List resource(s) you can use to find more uses of water.

1. _____

2. _____

3. _____

Did you know that water is used to get energy from the food you eat?

Africa Activities: "Waste Not, Want Not"

Computation

To understand how much—and how easily—water can be wasted in a day, a week, or a month, complete the following class project.

Fill a large plastic container with water. Carefully puncture a small hole in the bottom to allow one drop to fall per second. Put the container over a can or bucket to see how much water is lost in ten minutes.

Answer: _____

Knowing how many minutes there are in a day, calculate the water loss in just one day.

Answer: _____

Many households have this much loss through leaks. Multiply the water loss by just half the houses in your town or city, and you will be astounded by the amount of water waste. How much is it?

Answer: _____

When you understand the importance of water for the Earth's land and population, you will understand how precipitation, or the lack of it, affects and influences the lives of people around the world.

Africa Activities: What's the Difference?

Critical Thinking (Standards 1, 4, 6, 12, 15, 17, and 18)

The countries of the Sahara are unique in their desert characteristics. Perhaps the most unique is Egypt, with its rich civilization that arose in the earliest times, its ancient pyramids (the only Ancient World Wonder still in existence), and the longest river in the world, the Nile. The great diversities found in Africa can lead to many comparisons of different peoples, religions, languages, economies, and location. Addressing these differences brings about a greater understanding of the cultures of this continent.

Activity 1. Work in pairs to list the differences you find between Egypt and the Democratic Republic of Congo.

Egypt	Democratic Republic of Congo (DRC)
Located on the eastern side of Africa	Located on the western side of Africa
Egypt is primarily a Muslim country.	DRC is mostly Christian.

Choose two other countries, cities, rivers, or peoples of Africa. Do another exercise, and then exchange them with other students. Other ideas might be a Central African country compared with one of the island countries; an economically depressed country such as Liberia with one such as South Africa; or the Nile River compared with the Niger River.

Africa is one continent, but there are many differences in its countries, cities, and cultures. Work together to explore the differences.

From *Teaching Global Literacy Using Mnemonics* by Joan Ebbesmeyer.
Westport, CT: Libraries Unlimited/Teacher Ideas Press. Copyright © 2006.

Africa Activities: Crack the Code

Analyze and Synthesize

There are more than eight hundred languages spoken in Africa, and thus many different ways to communicate.

The ancient Egyptians used a form of writing called hieroglyphics. It is made up of pictures and symbols and was a mystery to modern man for a thousand years. The discovery of a carved stone (called the Rosetta Stone) by one of Napoleon's army officers was the key to the mystery of the long-forgotten language of ancient Egypt. A French officer discovered it in 1799, and a French scholar named Champollion learned the meaning of the Egyptian characters carved on the stone. The random symbols and pictures produced a code. Champollion cracked the code through his knowledge of Greek and the Egyptian language of his day (called Demotic). Deciphering this code opened up a much greater understanding of the culture of Ancient Egypt.

Example

A	B	C	D	E	F	G	H	I	J	K	L	M	N	O	P	Q	R	S	T	U	V	W	X	Y	Z
*	^	◆	@	+	=	>	%	~	●	(	#	!	|	\	▲	✗	<	:	•	¢	¡	£	■	→	†

Make a symbolic code for yourself and a friend. You can then send secret messages.

Letter	Code	Letter	Code
A		N	
B		O	
C		P	
D		Q	
E		R	
F		S	
G		T	
H		U	
I		V	
J		W	
K		X	
L		Y	
M		Z	

From *Teaching Global Literacy Using Mnemonics* by Joan Ebbesmeyer.
Westport, CT: Libraries Unlimited/Teacher Ideas Press. Copyright © 2006.

Africa Activities: Survival Is the Name of the Game

The main function of all cultures is learning to survive. Many African peoples have dealt with this over many decades. There are dangerous regions where starvation and lack of water, wild animals, Savannah fires, and terrorist tribes threaten the lives of people and animals alike.

We find animals in the countries of central Africa that are adapted by nature to defend themselves and be able to survive.

Look at the list of animals that follows and research the ways they defend themselves. How many more African animals can you add to this list?

Animal	Defenses		
Giraffe	Heavy hooves	Long legs	Great height
Wild boar			
Lion			
Zebra			
Rhinoceros			
Monkey			

From *Teaching Global Literacy Using Mnemonics* by Joan Ebbesmeyer.
Westport, CT: Libraries Unlimited/Teacher Ideas Press. Copyright © 2006.

Africa Activities: Deadly Defenses

Surviving in the jungle can be very difficult. What four defenses do you think are the best for surviving in such a dangerous place?

1. _____
2. _____
3. _____
4. _____

If you could combine those four defenses in one animal, what would it look like? What would you call this strange and wonderful creature?

Example:

1. Long, strong legs to run fast
2. Poison fangs to kill instantly
3. Hard shell to hide under
4. Long arms with sharp claws to climb quickly

You might be creating a giant turtle snake.

Can you draw an animal that might look like this? Use the space below, and be creative!

Chapter 7
Australia and Oceania

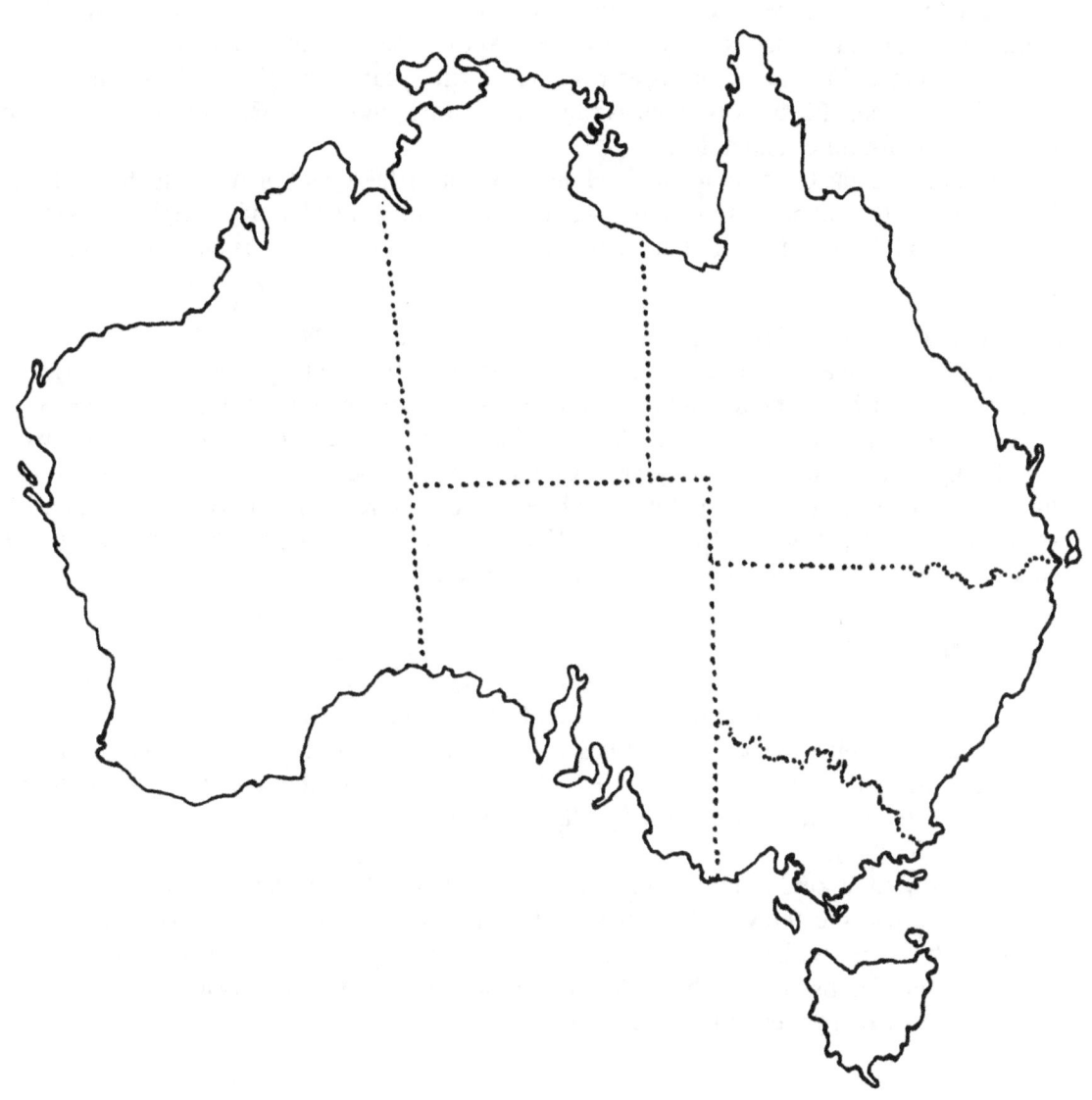

Australia and Oceania

Australia is a continent, a country, and an island that lies between the Indian and Pacific Oceans. Its land regions are made up of an interior of desert land called the Outback; surrounding this vast region are savanna grasslands, tropical rain forests, and cities. Ayers Rock, the Great Barrier Reef, the country's aboriginal (native) people, and the many unique species of animals—found nowhere else on Earth—make Australia unique and exciting!

Suggested Reading

Picture Books

Arnold, Marsha Diane. *The Pumpkin Runner.* Illustrated by Brad Sneed. Dial Books, 1998.

Joshua Summerhayes lives on a ten-thousand-acre sheep ranch in the Australian Outback. While others drive their jeeps or fly their planes to cover the vast areas of their ranchland, Joshua runs the distances instead. He has been running for fifty years, with Yellow Dog trailing behind him. The only thing he loves as much as running is eating pumpkins. The pumpkins give him the energy to run for miles and miles.

The big Koala-K race is Joshua's chance to win $10,000 and prove he is the best runner. No one thinks the old man can win the 542-mile race, but Joshua has a big supply of pumpkins; his best friend, Yellow Dog; and the will to win. This delightful story is based on a real-life experience.

Roth, Susan L. *The Biggest Frog in Australia.* Simon & Schuster, 1996.

Inspired by an aboriginal myth, this story tells of the biggest frog in Australia who awakens one day with the biggest thirst in the land. He drinks up all the puddles, lakes, and rivers on the continent. He can't stop until he has depleted the ocean and the rain clouds of all their water.

Being without any water, the plants begin to wilt, and the other animals are becoming very thirsty. Knowing they must think of something clever to force Frog to give up the water he has stored in his body, Wombat, Kookaburra, Kangaroo, and Koala all try their ideas, but with no success. The silly eels finally save the day for Australia!

Chapter Books

Cohn, Rachel. *The Steps.* Simon and Schuster Books for Young Readers, 2003.

Annabel is going to spend Christmas vacation with her father in Sydney, Australia. She is excited at the thought of leaving New York City for a while and about the many adventures that may await her. But she is concerned with how she will be received by her stepbrothers, stepsisters, and half-siblings.

It's a different kind of family and a different kind of life that she finds in this strange new land, but she learns to enjoy the happiness that comes from her extended family. Some of the adventures she shares with her stepsister are more than daring, but they both survive.

Annabelle learns to accept her father's happiness with his new family and knows she will be spending many more vacations in Australia.

Lester, Alison. *The Quicksand Pony.* Houghton Mifflin, 1997.

Ten-year-old Biddy loves her family, her pony Bella, and her wonderful life in the wild land of Australia. She has a life that is simple and orderly until the day she goes horseback riding on the beach and lands in the dangerous quicksand. Bella cannot free herself from the treacherous bog, and Biddy has to leave her as the tide comes in.

Biddy is sure she will never be happy again. But the next day the family finds footprints in the sand, along with human prints and the paw marks of a dog.

Someone had rescued the pony and taken her into the bush country! Biddy is determined to find out where they are. In doing so, she uncovers a mystery that has been puzzling the whole area for many years. Could a mother and her baby son have survived in the wild bush country for that length of time?

How the Little Devil Found a Home

A Mnemonic Story about Australia

Many thousands of years ago, there lived a small, savage animal that looked somewhat like a little bear. He had dark black fur with a few white spots and a large head atop his fat little body. He was called the "little devil" because of his atrocious habits—hiding in burrows all day and waiting until night to kill other unsuspecting animals.

This little animal lived on a very large island-continent called Australia with many other strange and unique animals, such as the platypus, wombat, dingo, and the frilled lizard, to name just a few.

These animals agreed with the King Kangaroo that the little devil must have a place of his very own. The little devil agreed, but where would that new home be?

Not knowing where to start, the group decided to search in every ***direction***. They drew up a map and divided the vast land into regions of *states* and *territories*. They traveled first to the northern area and, naturally, they called it **Northern Australia;** but it was too bare. So, turning west, they came to the vast land stretching from the northern to the southern boundary of the country, and they named it **Western Australia;** but it was too big! Moving to the east, they entered the land south of the Northern Territory and, of course, called it **South Australia.** The little devil liked the south but it was too big. So they divided it and called the new region New South Wales.

Hoping to settle things, the animals offered their enemy a small territory inside New South Wales that would be called **Australian Capital Territory,** and the little devil could be king of the capital! This really appealed to him, but there was land remaining, and he wanted to see it all before he made a decision.

The group had run out of direction names, so they called the land to the north and south of New South Wales after the former Queen of England. The queen is still the head of state in Australia. (The queen of Great Britain is also the queen of Australia but has little powers of government.) The huge northern part was called **Queensland,** and the southern land, named after a famous English queen, was called **Victoria.** However, the little devil could not make up his mind!

By this time, the group had had enough of this obnoxious animal! After showing him all the regions of the great island, country, and continent called Australia and extolling the virtues of the landscape including the steamy tropical rain forests, the swamps, deserts, and grasslands, he still remained undecided!

In desperation, the group gave him to the native people of Australia, the Aborigines. It didn't take long before they gave him right back! They tried to lose him in each one of the four great deserts—they tried the Great Sandy, the Great Victoria, the Simpson, and the Gibson, but he survived them all. They even put him on top of Ayers Rock—over a thousand feet high in the middle of the desert—but he made his way back to the group. They thought for sure they would be successful when they took him to the eastern coast and the high mountains called the Great Dividing Range and left him on top of the highest peak, Mount Kosiusko. No! They failed again. The little devil was quite good at mountain climbing.

The group was desperate. They had had all they could take! And so, they decided to rid the world of this pest once and for all. The ocean would solve their problem. Their first idea was to throw him off the eastern coast, but they thought he might find something on the Great Barrier Reef to get him back to shore. So they traveled as far south as they could go and threw him far out to sea.

From *Teaching Global Literacy Using Mnemonics* by Joan Ebbesmeyer.
Westport, CT: Libraries Unlimited/Teacher Ideas Press. Copyright © 2006.

In the end, the little devil proved to be the ultimate survivor by swimming until he reached an island. It was that island that he claimed as another state of Australia. He called it **TASMANIA,** and to this day he is known as the Tasmanian devil.

That is the way the six states and two territories of Australia were named. Just think of the directions (north, west, and two souths), the queen of England, and the famous Queen Victoria, and finally of the Tasmanian devil to remember them. We still know them as:

Northern Territory, Western Australia, South Australia, New South Wales, Australian Capital Territory (Canberra), Queensland, Victoria, and **Tasmania.**

Australia Activities: Sensational Similes

Creative Writing: Australia in Simile (Standards 2, 6, and 18)

Australia is unique in so many ways. It is the smallest continent, the only one that is both a country and an island as well. It is the only continent that is mostly desert land. It has animals found nowhere else on earth and is the only continent that lies completely below the equator. It has the largest coral reef in the world, too.

Fluency

How many other unique things can you list about Australia? Research and report your findings.

Flexibility

Now that you have researched Australia and are familiar with its people, places, and environments, try describing the wonders of this land in simile. You could create a book of interesting comparisons. Connect an adjective to the person, place, or animal; add a verb; and finish with a simile explaining where or how, to make creative sentences.

Simile

Example:
Add an adjective, a verb, a location or action, and a simile to the following. Here's an example:

1. The **awesome** Great Barrier Reef **protecting** the **eastern shore of Australia** **is like a silent, stone sentinel**.

Now try to fill in the blanks with adjectives, verbs, expansions, and similes.

2. The _____ Frilled Lizard _____
   is as _____ .

From Teaching Global Literacy Using Mnemonics *by Joan Ebbesmeyer.*
Westport, CT: Libraries Unlimited/Teacher Ideas Press. Copyright © 2006.

Australia and Oceania 125

3. The _____ Ayers Rock _____

   is like _____.

4. The _____ Australian Desert _____

   is as _____.

5. The _____ Aborigine _____

   is like _____.

6. The _____ Lake Eyre _____

   is like _____.

7. The _____ Dingo _____

   is as _____.

8. The white-sailed Opera House welcoming all who enter Sydney Harbor

   is like a great earth-bound ship.

9. The _____ Mount Kosiusko _____

   is like _____.

From *Teaching Global Literacy Using Mnemonics* by Joan Ebbesmeyer.
Westport, CT: Libraries Unlimited/Teacher Ideas Press. Copyright © 2006.

Australia Activities: Awesome Animals of Australia

Science (Standards 2, 9, and 15)

Millions of years ago the land bridge between Asia and Australia disappeared, which caused the animal life in Australia to evolve independent of those on the Asian continent. This produced many strange and unique animals that can be found nowhere else on Earth.

Work in groups as you learn about these animals and see how many you can list from A to Z.

Apostle Bird	J_____	S_____
B_____	Kookaburra	T_____
C_____	L_____	U_____
D_____	M_____	V_____
Echidna	N_____	Wandering Albatross
F_____	O_____	X_____
G_____	Platypus	Y_____
H_____	Q_____	Z_____
I_____	R_____	

Elaboration

Make your list of animals more creative by expanding into sentences using "alliteration." Alliteration is the repetition of beginning sounds in neighboring words of two or more, such as the phrases "Wild West" and "Big Bang."

D: Dingos don't dawdle in the dangerous desert.

K: Kangaroos can kick koalas clear across the continent.

C: Cassowarys can't compete with canaries who can fly!

How many can you add to this list of alliterative sentences?

What's the Sense of It?

Science: Using Your Senses (Standards 3, 5, 10, and 14)

To know Australia is to love and enjoy it. You must use all your senses to become familiar with, and remember, this vast and exciting land.

To report on what you have learned, make a list of all the *unique* people, places, and things that define Australia. List things that you can find nowhere else on Earth.

Great Barrier Reef	Lake Eyre	Murray River	Ayers Rock	Aborigines
Kangaroos	Dingos	Sydney Opera House	Outback	James Cook

Add as many things as you can to the list.

Pick the thing you find most unique and interesting. Report on it through *the five senses.*

Example: The Australian Desert

I make up about two-thirds of the entire land region of this continent. You will find that I am mostly wilderness, with the Great Victorian deserts, the Gibson and the Great Sandy Desert. I have saltpans, rocky outcrops, and dried-out lakes. I am hot and harsh, but I'm home to many animals and native people.

Here I *see:*

The Australian Aborigine people who have survived my harsh land by becoming expert hunters and learning to live in this desert land and by moving from place to place in search of water. I see the great Macdonnell and Musgrave mountain ranges, and I see the striking colors on the mountain walls as the sunlight changes and I gaze at the majesty of Uluru (the Aborigine's name for Ayres Rock), which towers more than one thousand feet into the air, above the flat desert land of the Northern Territory.

From *Teaching Global Literacy Using Mnemonics* by Joan Ebbesmeyer.
Westport, CT: Libraries Unlimited/Teacher Ideas Press. Copyright © 2006.

Here I *listen* to:
The bark of the wild dingo dog, the loud braying call of the kookaburra, and the lyrebird's song, which imitates the sounds that many other birds make—something only the lyrebird can do.

I hear the English words spoken by most Australians and the tongue-twisting sounds of the words spoken by the Aborigines. I hear the drone of small planes flying over my vast land, as they carry ranchers from one station to another.

Here I *smell*: The acrid odor of smoke from the bushfires caused from a single spark, and the blazing fire rising high in the dry Outback of Australia. I yearn to smell the sweet vineyards that will produce the wines of South Australia and also to smell the tropical fruits, pineapple, bananas, and sugarcane from the hot, moist state of Queensland.

Here I *taste*:
The hot winds that blow across the flat desert of the Northern Territory, the endless sand and scrub bushes that cover the land. The sheep taste the saltbush in times of drought, and their leaves can sustain these animals for a year with nothing else to eat.

Here I *touch*:
I must touch the soft wool of the sheep, sheared on the vast ranches. These ranches stretch thousands of square miles across the land. Then, I will travel farther to taste the saltwater from the many seas that surround this great continent and touch the wild open ocean.

What will you report on through your senses? It could be the Great Barrier Reef, the Sydney Opera House, or the prison colony, which began the colonization of Australia in the late 1700s. So much to choose from!

Map of Oceania

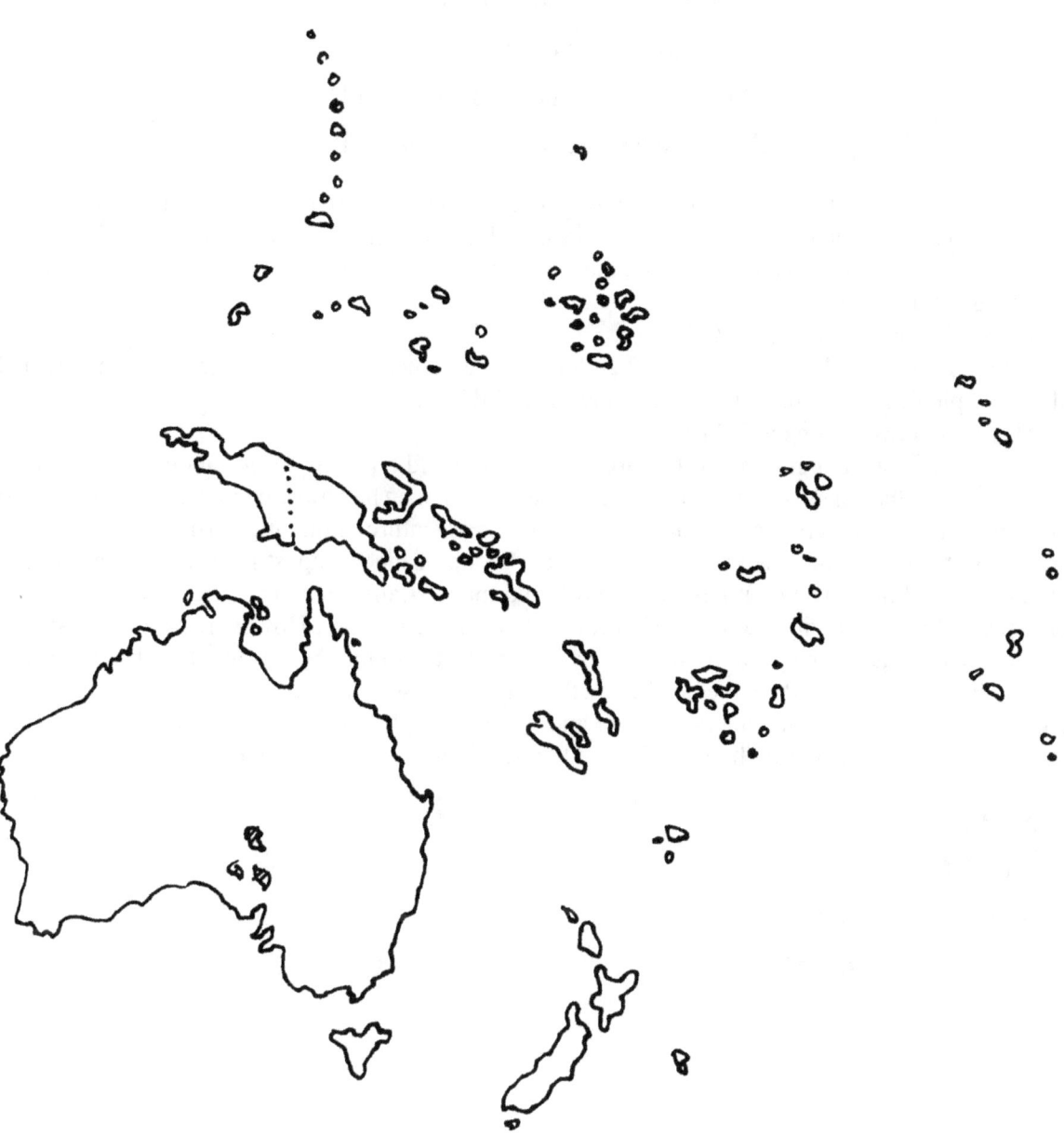

Nauru and the Island of the Stone Head

A Mnemonic Story about Oceania

Islands here and islands there,

Islands, islands everywhere,

Some are large and some are small,

Some have stone heads standing tall.

This is the story of Nauru, who lived many thousands of years ago. He lived on a large island, situated in the largest ocean in the world. We now call this ocean the Pacific. Nauru loved his island home, but he longed to see what lay beyond the watery horizon. He thought of it all day, as he worked from dawn 'til dark. He had to work hard to survive.

There was never a time to **NAP!**

All the island people worked hard. They hunted and gathered food from the land. They fished and did simple farming to feed themselves and their children.

There was never a time to **NAP!**

Sometimes, late at night around the fire, the elders would tell their stories about the new lands and islands that others had ventured to long ago. These brave men had traveled in their open canoes to search the unknown waters for new lands. What a great adventure, thought Nauru!

Finally the day came when Nauru convinced a group of the strongest men to sail with him in search of a new home. They journeyed far and found many strange islands in the vast ocean. They tasted exotic foods and witnessed animals they had never seen before. However, they never stayed very long in any place—that is, until they discovered the island of the mysterious stone heads (Easter Island). There were hundreds of the heads, and they stood like sentinels, circling the island and looking out to sea. Nauru and the others felt safe and happy with the stone heads to guard the land for them. They stayed in their new home and were happy when they found time every day for a

NAP!!

N for **NEW ZEALAND**

A for **AUSTRALIA**

P for **PACIFIC ISLANDS**

From *Teaching Global Literacy Using Mnemonics* by Joan Ebbesmeyer.
Westport, CT: Libraries Unlimited/Teacher Ideas Press. Copyright © 2006.

Chapter 8

Antarctica

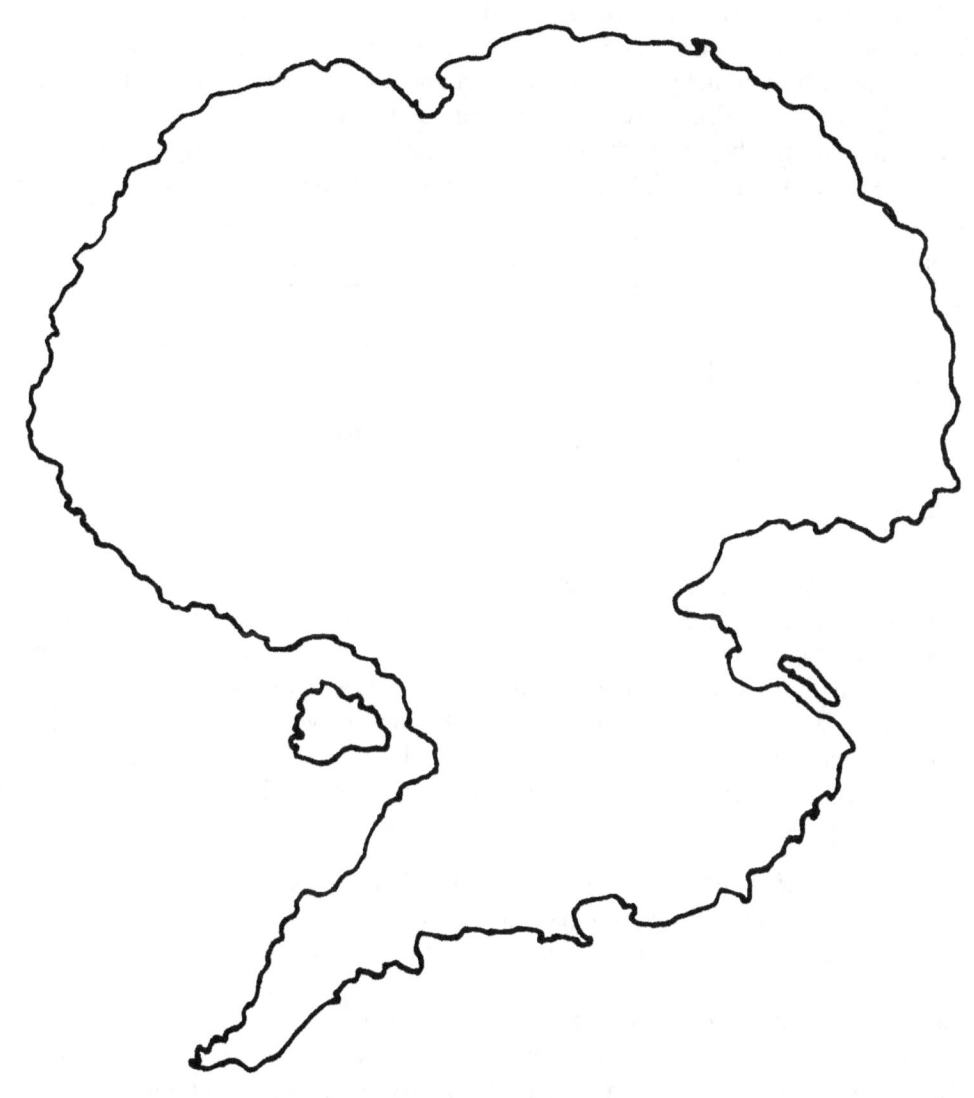

Antarctica

The fifth largest continent on Earth is located at the bottom of the world. It is called Antarctica; it is a wasteland of snow and ice to some people, while others view it as alive with history, color, and life!

Here we find the coldest region on Earth! It is situated on the southernmost point of our world and covers 5.5 million square miles of frozen land. The sun never rises for half of the year, and it never sets for the other half. Only scientists and a few visitors live there, and then only for a period time. There are no permanent human residents. The penguins are the only creatures that seem to appreciate this hostile land, where temperatures can measure less than 100 degrees below zero (Fahrenheit) and the ice can be more than 6,000 feet thick in some places. *But*:

Some think Antarctica is the biggest story in geography today! That's because of the warning coming from many scientists and environmentalists about global warming. Will this continent's ice melt lead to the destruction of life on Earth? Educators can review the national standards on activity sheets and lead students to an understanding of all the issues involved in global warming, showing how physical and human systems play a role, as well as how the environment and societies will be affected. As educators and learners, we need to be more aware of connections between all things.

Finally, to gain additional insight into Antarctica and its only native inhabitants, the penguins, see the film *The March of the Penguins*. It's almost unbelievable!

In the activities for this chapter, note that "Are We Heating Up?" is for upper grades and "Poles Apart" is designed for lower grades. Following are the answers to the final activity, "Fact or Fiction."

| 1. Fiction | 2. Fiction | 3. Fact | 4. Fiction | 5. Fiction |
| 6. Fiction | 7. Fact | 8. Fact | 9. Fact | 10. Fiction |

Suggested Reading

Picture Books

Cowcher, Helen. *Antarctica.* Farrar, Straus & Giroux, 1990.

>The penguin is one of the few animals that can endure the frozen cold of the South Pole. In this book we see the many dangers that threaten their existence. The peril is constant and only with the complete family, and other penguins, can there be any hope of survival. The vigilance is never-ending, as winter storms threaten the life of penguins young and old. Even the penguins that are not hatched are at the mercy of ferocious seals and hungry skua birds.
>
>These are the ancient enemies, and now there is another one. This one can arrive in planes or in ships. And this enemy could be the greatest danger of all!

Lee, Sandra Crow. *Penguins and Polar Bears.* National Geographic, 1985.

>Two of the most interesting animals of the arctic regions are graphically described in this book. It shows their surprising commonalties, even though one is a huge mammal, and the other a relatively small bird!
>
>The dangers, beauty, excitement, and wonder of the two poles are described as vast deserts, where the water is forever frozen! Life is harsh and unyielding at both ends of Earth, yet these animals, who best exemplify the regions, are evidently comfortable in their environment.

Swan, Robert. *Destination Antarctica.* Scholastic, 1988.

Robert Scott was an intrepid explorer, and his dream was to be the first one to reach the South Pole. The hazardous expedition would take him and his men across hundreds of miles of snow and ice. There would be darkness, danger, loneliness, boredom, and unbelievable cold to keep them company along the way. Can you imagine the disappointment of reaching the destination, only to find that someone else had beaten them to the prize by just five short weeks? Not only did they lose the race, they lost their lives in a snowstorm and remain there in icy graves to this day.

This book is about another Robert, Robert Swan, who decides to follow the seventy-four-year-old trail to Antarctica under the same primitive conditions as Scott and his men. Their struggle is an exciting story to read! Who *was* the first man to reach the South Pole?

Tillotson, Katherine. *Penguin and Little Blue.* Atheneum Books, 2005.

Here is a picture book that will make you laugh while providing information about the continent of Antarctica and the penguins that live there. Penguin and his friend, Little Blue, are featured performers for Water World in San Francisco. They are provided with the best of everything, but all they want is to go back home. The two share many adventures on plane rides (because they can't fly) and in hotel rooms when they order krill for lunch and find enough water and ice to make a miniature South Pole. After informing the reader of many Antarctic facts, they finally find a creative way to return to their homeland.

Chapter Books

Bledsoe, Lucy Jane. *The Antarctic Scoop.* Holiday House Books, 2003.

Victoria is only twelve years old, but she is weighed down by many disappointments and problems. Children should have parents to depend on, but Victoria's parents are more caught up in their own breakup. Her classmates look on her as an alien because of her great love of astronomy. She has also found that New York, with all its tall buildings, is not a good place to study the stars.

When an opportunity comes for Victoria to visit Antarctica, she doesn't take long to make up her mind to go. What an adventure! She finds excitement in another world, the South Pole. But she also experiences danger. Best of all, she finds "Alexander the Great"!

Dixon, Franklin W. *The Stone Idol.* Simon & Shuster, 1981.

There is a theft of government material in Antarctica, and the Hardy boys are traveling south to solve the mystery. Their adventures take them to many regions connected to the South Pole. They follow a clue that leads them to the Andes Mountains, where they face real danger with desperate criminals.

The boys escape and fly off to the Antarctic to join their father in searching for a valuable sculpture. Their final destination is Easter Island, where a birdman threatens their lives. They must uncover the last clue, the clue to the stone idol!

Antarctica Activities: What's in a Name?

Environment and Society: Standards 11–15

Several countries have claimed sections of Antarctica because of possible mineral wealth beneath the ice and snow. However, an international treaty prevents mining, because it could destroy the Earth's ecosystems. The world's nations have shown an unusual willingness to work together to conserve nature and the planet, Earth!

To appreciate a person, place, or thing, we must first know something about it. Before reading several picture books on penguins, we might think of the seventeen kinds, or species, of penguins that are hardy enough to live in the harsh, cold land of Antarctica. There are names for every species of penguin, and reasons for the names they were given. Look at some of the names listed below and write why you think they were named that way. Take a guess if you don't know, then research to find out if you were correct.

Penguin Species of Antarctica

1. Emperor _____
   _____
2. Chinstrap _____
   _____
3. Little Blue _____
   _____
4. King _____
   _____
5. Yellow-eyed _____
   _____
6. Macaroni _____
   _____

From *Teaching Global Literacy Using Mnemonics* by Joan Ebbesmeyer.
Westport, CT: Libraries Unlimited/Teacher Ideas Press. Copyright © 2006.

Antarctica Activities: Penguin Problems

Problem Solving

List all the problems you have learned that threaten the penguins in Antarctica.

_____
_____
_____
_____
_____

Which one do you consider to be the animals' biggest problem?

_____

List possible ways to solve the problem.

_____
_____
_____
_____
_____

What things must you take into consideration when trying to solve a problem such as this? (Examples: too expensive; may be impossible)

Some people have said this about conserving Earth: "We make the greatest mistake when we realize we can do little to solve the problem, so we do nothing at all." What do you think this statement means?

_____
_____
_____

From *Teaching Global Literacy Using Mnemonics* by Joan Ebbesmeyer.
Westport, CT: Libraries Unlimited/Teacher Ideas Press. Copyright © 2006.

Antarctica Activities: Adapt or Die

As we see in Helen Cowcher's book *Antarctica,* many penguins are ***apt*** to die in the perilous cold land of Antarctica. However, like all mothers, Mother Nature will protect life whenever possible. She does this by being able to ***add*** something to overcome the possibility of death and destruction. All animals, including human, must learn to adapt to survive.

Listed below are the dangerous "apts" that can lead to death for the penguins. Research the penguin and "add" what Mother Nature provides to allow animals to "ad-apt" to survive.

Apt	Add
To freeze in the winter storm	A thick layer of blubber for insulation
To be killed by the ferocious leopard seal	
To be eaten by the swooping skua birds	
To starve while guarding the eggs	
To be annihilated by humans	
To be chased by a killer whale	

From *Teaching Global Literacy Using Mnemonics* by Joan Ebbesmeyer.
Westport, CT: Libraries Unlimited/Teacher Ideas Press. Copyright © 2006.

Antarctica Activities: Maps

The simple map below gives you an idea of the immensity of Antarctica, with the oceans and nearest land masses above it.

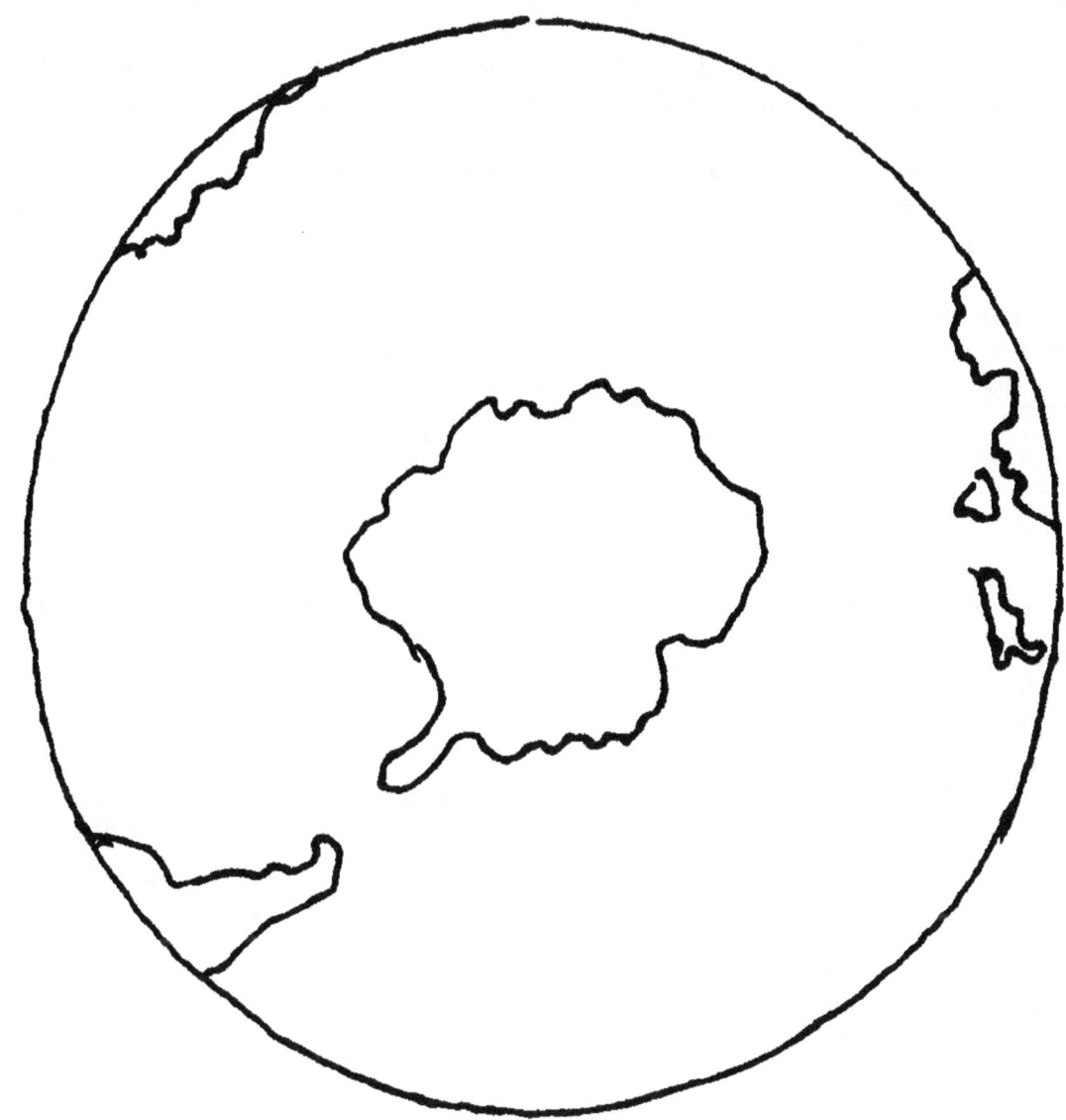

Antarctica Activities: Persons, Places, and Things

Vocabulary

The study and research of Antarctica can introduce many unfamiliar vocabulary words. Getting to know and use these words will give a better insight and understanding of the region, culture, and people we are studying.

The words below are connected to Antarctica. Research the continent and place them in the right columns under People, Places, Animals, or Things. Be ready to explain your answers.

McMurdo	skua	lichens	Amundsen	gale	terrain
Rockhopper	ice-breakers	liverworts	baleen	cormorants	Scott Adelie
sea lion	creches	rookery	brood	pouch	blubber
Ross	Ice Shelf	sastrugi			

People	Places	Animals	Things

From *Teaching Global Literacy Using Mnemonics* by Joan Ebbesmeyer.
Westport, CT: Libraries Unlimited/Teacher Ideas Press. Copyright © 2006.

Antarctica Activities: Poles Apart

Antarctica is a continent because it is a large area of land. It is also a pole, the South Pole. Our other pole, the North Pole, is *not* a continent. It is a vast ocean surrounded by land. Much of the ocean is frozen throughout the year.

Contrast and Compare: The North and South Poles

Think of all the ways the North Pole and the South Pole are alike or different. Some ideas were given in the information above. What others can you find?

Alike
Both are at ends of the Earth.
Both are cold and covered with ice and snow.
Different
The North Pole has polar bears, the South Pole has penguins.
The North Pole is at the top of Earth, the South Pole is at the bottom.

From *Teaching Global Literacy Using Mnemonics* by Joan Ebbesmeyer.
Westport, CT: Libraries Unlimited/Teacher Ideas Press. Copyright © 2006.

Antarctica Activities: Are We Heating Up?

Research (Standards 11–16)

1. Read the intriguing seventy-four-page article in the September 2004 issue of *National Geographic* magazine. It is the first of a three-part series.

    The world *is* warming up. Many scientists believe this to be a fact.
    What do you think is our biggest concern because of global warming? Is it floods, famine, lost ecosystems, drought, fire, or extinction?

2. Work in groups to convince the rest of the class what is the biggest concern about global warming, and what it means for the future—your future!

3. Include a problem-solving plan to stop or slow global warming. Send it to your senators and representatives. Remember: it's *your* future we're talking about!

Plan:

_____

_____

_____

_____

_____

_____

_____

_____

_____

_____

_____

_____

From *Teaching Global Literacy Using Mnemonics* by Joan Ebbesmeyer.
Westport, CT: Libraries Unlimited/Teacher Ideas Press. Copyright © 2006.

Antarctic Activities: Imagery (Standards 7 and 10)

After researching and reading about the vast, unique world of Antarctica, ask students to sit quietly and close their minds to all thoughts but the beautiful landscape, animals, and climate of the continent. They might want to close their eyes to visualize the scene as you slowly read the following:

The setting sun glides lower and lower, finally sinking into the shimmering whiteness of the ice-covered mountains. A mist settles over the vastness, creating a fantasy world of blue and white. The glacier sparkles in the fading sunlight as it slowly, slowly seeks the sea below. The sharp, icy wind has no barrier in its way as it sweeps endlessly across the frozen land. At times there is the alien, cracking sound of the great Russian icebreaker as it plows itself through the savage ice of the sea or the screech of the skua birds as they prey on the gulls and penguins. But usually there is silence, a serenity that reaches to your very soul.

Antarctic Activities: Imagine That!

After creating an image of Antarctica in your mind, read the three columns below and choose *one phrase* from each of the three columns to put together into a "simile sentence." Pick the combination of phrases that you think will make a good, creative sentence.

Example

The glorious beauty	of the arctic land	is like a pristine paradise.

The utter loneliness	of the savage snowstorm	is like a fading dream.
The lingering sadness	of the snowy mountain	is like a lost love.
The glorious beauty	of the icy wind	is like a falling tear.
The awesome majesty	of the arctic land	is like a raging beast.
The unseen danger	of the unyielding wilderness	is like a pristine paradise.

Can you add to the following phrases to create your own similes?

The everlasting image	of the frozen sea	is like_____.
The_____	of the swooping skua	is like a shrieking nightmare.
The utter remoteness	of the _____	is like an alien world.

Now use your simile sentences to write a creative paragraph on Antarctica on the back of this worksheet.

From *Teaching Global Literacy Using Mnemonics* by Joan Ebbesmeyer.
Westport, CT: Libraries Unlimited/Teacher Ideas Press. Copyright © 2006.

Antarctic Activities: Fact or Fiction

Mark **fact** or **fiction** behind each statement. Be ready to defend your answers.

1. Antarctica has only a small human population living there permanently.
   _____

2. Because the ground is always frozen, scientists learn little about Antarctica.
   _____

3. The large amount of plankton in the Antarctic Ocean turns the water a bright green.
   _____

4. There are about as many plants in Antarctica as there are in the Arctic.
   _____

5. The polar bear is the most common animal of the Antarctic.
   _____

6. The Antarctic is smaller than the Arctic.
   _____

7. Amundsen was the first human to reach the Antarctic.
   _____

8. Emperor penguins can live without food for two months.
   _____

9. The emperor penguin lays only one egg per year.
   _____

10. The Antarctic region receives large snowfalls each year.
    _____

From Teaching Global Literacy Using Mnemonics by Joan Ebbesmeyer.
Westport, CT: Libraries Unlimited/Teacher Ideas Press. Copyright © 2006.

Chapter 9

Asia

Asia

Think of the size of Earth's entire land area.

Asia occupies one-third of that land!

Think of the billions of people who live on the earth.

Asia is home to more than half of them!

This is true even though much of Asia is uninhabited! People cannot live in the tundra (cold, treeless land) of the far northern regions or in the large areas of parched desert and high mountains of the central regions.

Asia is the largest of the world's seven continents, reaching from the Arctic Circle in the north to the islands of Indonesia in the south. It stretches from the island of Cyprus in the west to the islands of Japan in the east. Asia is in close proximity to every continent in the world, with the exception of South America. It borders Antarctica on the north, and Europe and Africa to the west. Australia lies to the south, and a short stretch of the Bering Straight separates Asia from North America.

Asia is a land of great variety, from the high and low (Himalayan Mountains versus the Dead Sea), cold and hot (Arctic Russia versus tropical Indonesia) to the many languages (from Arabic to Chinese), the wet and dry (the deserts of Syria versus rainy Bangladesh), and a multiformity of cultures (from the ancient land of China to the oil-rich Arab nations). It is an amazing and diverse continent!

Suggested Reading

Many books have been written and illustrated about the countries of Asia. The two mentioned here could serve as lures to get young—and older—students interested in learning more about the largest continent in the world. *Teachers should not hesitate to use picture books to motivate interest in their students at every age and grade level.* Many of today's picture books are beautifully illustrated and contain good information. They may serve to involve reluctant learners in expanding and researching a challenging subject, and also serve as a springboard to deeper investigations in the study of the world.

Larin, Anne. *Perfect Crane*. HarperCollins, 1981.
   The art of Japanese paper folding is illustrated in this story of Gami, the magician. Gami creates a perfect paper crane and then brings it to life, only to find that the only way you can keep something you love is to set it free.

Lattimore, Deborah Norse. *The Dragon's Robe*. HarperCollins, 1990.
   The story weaves a tale of the culture of China, where the dragon is revered as a symbol of good luck. In the story, Kwan Yin creates a robe for the Chinese emperor and teaches him a lesson of honor and goodness.

Lee, Cynthia Chin. *A Is for Asia*. Illustrated by Yumi Heo. Orchard Books, 1997.
   The book uses the alphabet to introduce many aspects of Asian localities, climates, peoples, animals, art forms, and cultures. Every letter and page can be used to expand into in-depth research of Asian countries, philosophies, ancient civilizations, religions, and more. It's a great book to use as an assessment tool; have students create their own "A to Z Book" as they explore the five main regions of this vast continent: the Russian Federation, Southwest Asia, Southern Asia, Eastern Asia, and Southeast Asia.

Newton, Pam. *The Stonecutter.* A Folktale from India. G. P. Putnam & Sons, 1990.

>Be careful of what you wish for—it might come true!

>The poor stonecutter of India wishes for many things in his quest for wealth and power, only to find that what he was, and what he had before all the wishes, was the best of what he could ever be!

Reynolds, Jan. *Himalaya—Vanishing Cultures.* Harcourt Brace Jovanovich, 1991.

>The Sherpa and the Tibetans are the peoples of the Himalayan Mountain region. We find that they are much like we are—they enjoy festivals with sweet treats and dancing. The children go to school while the parents work hard to provide for the family. Life can be difficult, however, trying to live within the world's highest mountain system. The climate can be harsh in the cold mountains, and yaks (large shaggy animals) must be used to carry trade goods across the mountains. Nevertheless, the people find happiness in their simple life and fulfill their needs for a comfortable life through bartering (trading) with others.

Sayre, April Pulley. *Greetings, Asia.* Millbrook Press, 2003.

>A wonderful introduction to Asia that includes the people, plants, animals, landforms, climates, and geography of this large and multifaceted continent. This book can be used to assign research into the many areas of this vast continent.

>A section of the classroom could be used for all the books collected on the various areas to be studied. In addition, many books are available to interest students in the countries and five main regions of the vast continent.

>Some additional books that could lure readers into an expanded research of the diverse peoples, regions and cultures follow.

Asia Activities: Learning the World

In this last section of "learning the world" through storytelling and mnemonics, students should be encouraged to start thinking of their own creative games, rhymes, and mind tricks to remember geography facts. Asia is a challenging continent for practicing the skills. The students could work in groups, and their best ideas can be taught to other classes. (Teaching is a great way to learn!)

Teachers must serve as mentors in this process and be creative in thinking of "lures and prompts" when students need them. (More on lures and prompts follows later in the chapter.)

The maps and activities on the following pages will give you a start in learning the localities, countries, and cultures of the five main zones of Asia.

148 Teaching Global Literacy Using Mnemonics

1. **The Russian Federation (Some Countries Are Part of Europe)**

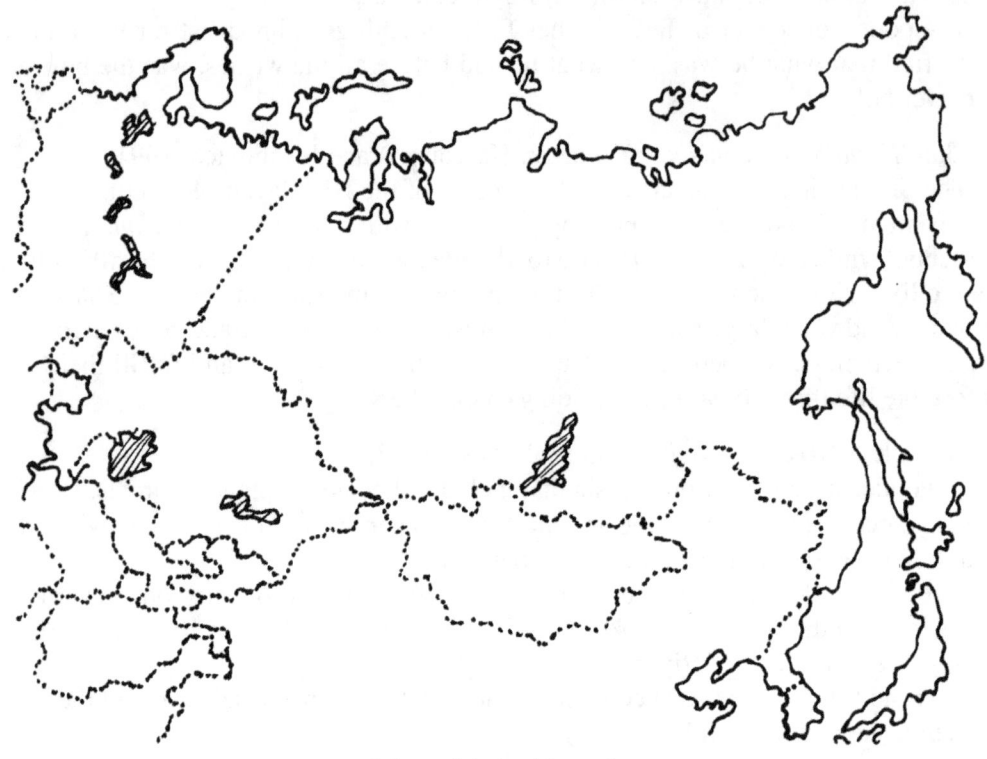

Map of Asia, Zone 1

2. **Southwest Asia (Saudi Arabia and Surrounding Countries)**

Map of Asia, Zone 2

3. **Southern Asia (India and Surrounding Countries)**

Map of Asia, Zone 3

4. **Eastern Asia (China and Surrounding Countries, Including Japan)**

Map of Asia, Zone 4

150 Teaching Global Literacy Using Mnemonics

5. Southeast Asia (Large Peninsula of Countries, Including the Islands of Indonesia)

Map of Asia, Zone 5

Prompt—Asian Alliteration (Standards 3–6)

Have a large, unlabeled map of Asia in one part of the classroom, and each student will have a map or atlas and a thesaurus. As various Asian countries are discovered, discussed, and researched, students can begin labeling the countries on the large, common map and creating their own book, *Asian Alliteration*.

Older students should be encouraged to make their sentences as *defining and meaningful* as possible. This activity can be ongoing or a culmination of Asian study.

Younger students might only be asked to find an Asian country, river, mountain, or desert to put next to each letter.

Asia Activities: A to Z

How many sentences with words beginning with the same first letter can you create?

A. Armenia, Azerbaijan, and Afghanistan are all in Asia.

B. Bangladesh is between Bhutan and Burma (Myanmar).

C.

D. Deadly dehydration is found in the dry deserts of Asia.

E.

F.

G.

H.

I. India and Indonesia, Iraq and Iran, are all near the Indian Ocean.

J.

K.

L.

M.

N.

O. Oman overlooks the Indian Ocean.

P.

Q.

R.

S. Syria (and also Cyprus) is smaller, with lower standards, than southwest Saudi Arabia.

T.

U.

V.

W.

X. eXcellent eXamples of eXceptional eXcavations can be found in ancient Asia.

Y.

Z. Zoom to the zenith of a ziggurat to see all over ancient Asia.

Asia Activities: Lure

Rhymes to Remember (Standards 12 and 13)

After the Cold War ended, the former Soviet Union (now the Russian Federation) cooperated with people who lived in the Eurasian parts of the lands it had occupied earlier in the twentieth century. These places wanted to be independent countries, free of Soviet control, and new nations were formed. These Eurasian countries have names that are unfamiliar to some and may be difficult to remember for most students.

A mnemonic rhyme could help!

The eight countries are:

Armenia	Azerbaijan
Kazakhstan	Kyrgyzstan
Turkmenistan	Tajikistan
Uzbekistan	Georgia

After the students have heard and used the names several times, they may remember them with a simple rhyme.

A-A, K-K

T-T, U-G

A-A Armenia and Azerbaijan

K-K Kazakhstan and Kyrgyzstan

T-T Turkmenistan and Tajikistan

U-G Uzbekistan and Georgia

This would be a good time to encourage students to create a mnemonic of their own. They might write a short story about how the "Stan" family became connected to India. It helps them remember the countries above—Kazakhstan, Turkmenistan, Kyrgyzstan, Tajikistan, Uzbekistan—in addition to Pakistan and Afghanistan.

Prompt

Visualization (Standards 2, 3, 13–16)

1. Sometimes, visualization helps students to retain the names of unfamiliar places. I have asked students to visualize

    a sheik in Saudi Arabia cheering, "Yeah Man, Oh Man," as he watched Arabs unite and play the guitar in the rain as they traveled to Kuwait.

154 Teaching Global Literacy Using Mnemonics

This mind picture helped them to remember the countries surrounding Saudi Arabia—namely:

Yemen, Oman, United Arab Emirates, Qatar, Bahrain, and **Kuwait.**

2. To help remember locations, my students visualized the huge mountain of **Russia** pushing the rock of **Mongolia** into the head of **China.**

3. Stories of our brave soldiers in the Vietnam and Iraq wars can lead to learning and remembering the locations of these countries and the ones bordering them.

4. Students are fascinated by picture books on tsunamis. Current events on the devastating tsunami that affected **Indonesia, India, Sri Lanka,** and the **Maldives** in 2004 will likely make them aware of this part of the world.

Picture Books, Art, Analysis, and Assessment (Standards 3, 4, 10, and 11)

1. Books on **Japan** can lead to an interest in origami art or Haiku poetry. The book *Himalaya* could lead to the creation of masks and dances to use in a festival patterned after the people of **Tibet.**

2. In learning about the sturdy rock houses of the Himalayan people and the yurts (round tents) of the desert people of Iran, begin to analyze what shelters people of different areas of the world need for survival.

Answers to the activity on the next page are as follows:

1. J	2. E	3. G	4. M	5. A	6. B	7. I
8. K	9. N	10. D	11. F	12. C	13. L	14. H

Asia Activities: Home Sweet Home

Match the shelters with the people who live or lived in them. Place the correct letter next to the type of shelter.

1.	Mud huts _____	A.	Inuit (Eskimos)
2.	Palm branch house _____	B.	Wealthy Romans
3.	Sampans _____	C.	Pharaohs of Ancient Egypt
4.	Straw round houses _____	D.	Prehistoric tribes
5.	Igloos _____	E.	Jungle tribes of South America
6.	Villas _____	F.	Peasants in medieval times
7.	Castles _____	G.	China's water people
8.	Camp wagons _____	H.	Bedouins (Arab desert tribes)
9.	Underground houses _____	I.	Kings in medieval times
10.	Caves _____	J.	North African tribes
11.	Cottages _____	K.	Gypsies (the Roma people)
12.	Palaces _____	L.	Desert peoples of Iran
13.	Yurts _____	M.	Bushmen of the Kalahari
14.	Tents _____	N.	Saharan desert tribes

From *Teaching Global Literacy Using Mnemonics* by Joan Ebbesmeyer.
Westport, CT: Libraries Unlimited/Teacher Ideas Press. Copyright © 2006.

Asia Activity: Rhymes

Creativity

As students become familiar with countries, rivers, mountains, and landmarks of the areas of Asia, some will enjoy creating couplets to test the knowledge of their classmates. They could hold a "Competition of Couplets" or make a booklet for the library. The following are all couplets written by sixth-grade students.

Examples

I am the largest country of all!

I was the USSR before the fall.

(Russia)

I am small and in between

My people, the Mongols, are fierce and keen.

(Mongolia)

This country is one where our brave soldiers did fall,

For a memorial, we built them a wall.

(Vietnam)

I'm a small country, you might have heard

Putting "Boo" and "Tan" together will give the word.

(Bhutan)

Assessment (Could Involve All Eighteen Standards)

Reversing the role of student and teacher and involving the use of competition can lead to a fun way to learn. Students work alone, in pairs, or in groups to display their grasp and knowledge of the subject matter.

Groups can create Quiz Bowl competitions as they challenge one another to earn the most points for correct answers. In five-clue games, students are given five clues to guess an answer. Five points are earned for the first and most difficult clue, four for the second, less difficult clue, and so on. Student groups create their own quiz questions.

Examples

Asia Quiz

1. I am a desert country in southwest Asia.
2. I am directly south of Turkey.
3. My capitol is Nicosia.
4. I am a small island country.
5. I am located in the Mediterranean Sea.

Answer: Cyprus

1. I am a gulf in Southwest Asia.
2. I am situated between Saudi Arabia and Iran.
3. I am very important to the economy of the region.
4. Many tankers of oil travel on me.
5. I flow into the Arabian Sea.

Answer: Persian Gulf

1. I am a very small Asian country.
2. I lie between India and China.
3. I have the highest mountain peak in the world.
4. My capital is Katmandu, and my flag is unique.
5. I border Bhutan on the east.

Answer: Nepal

In creating these lures and prompts and in practicing fun ways such as storytelling and mnemonics for increasing global literacy, both teachers and students can find endless ways to expand their knowledge of the Earth and be able to retain the knowledge and information that is so vital in today's global community.

Good luck and have fun!!

Index

A Is for Asia, 147
Ada, Alma Flor, 47
Adams, Jan, 60
Africa, 105–18
   activities, 112–18
   Central, 109
   maps of, 105, 108, 109, 110
   mnemonic story about, 108–10
   Northern, 108
   Southern, 110
   suggested reading, 106–7
African Dream, 106
All the Children Were Sent Away, 90
Alliteration activities, 151, 152
America My Land Your Land Our Land, 2
Analogy activities, 52
Analysis, 65, 116
Anderson, Margaret J., 61
Antarctic Scoop, The, 133
Antarctica, 131–43
   maps of, 131, 137
Antarctica, 132
Arizona, 39
Arnold, Marsha Diane, 120
Art activities, 50, 71, 72, 73, 154
Asia, 145–57
   activities, 148–57
   maps, 145, 148–50
   suggested reading, 146–7
Assessment ideas and activities, 53–55, 100–3, 156–7
Atlas, using, 95
Attribute thinking, 65
Australia, 119–28
   activities, 124–8
   map, 119
   mnemonic story about, 122–3
   suggested reading, 120–1

Biggest Frog in Australia, The, 120
Bledsoe, Lucy Jane, 133
Book, creating, 39

Brown, Margaret Wise, 64
Buchanan, Dawn Lisa, 61
By the Hanukkah Light, 90

Cabot, John, 64
Call of the Wild, The, 68
Canada, 59–74
   activities, 64–74
   map, 59
   mnemonic stories for, 62–63, 74
   provinces of, 62–63
   suggested reading, 60–61
Captive, The, 107
Central America, 45–55
   activities for, 50–55
   map, 45
   mnemonic story about, 49
   suggested reading, 47–48
Cherry, Lynne, 76
Clayton, Bess, 107
Clue Question Games, 53–54, 101–2, 103
Code, cracking, 116
Cohn, Rachel, 120
Compare and contrast activities, 81–82, 98, 139
Computation activity, 114
Cowcher, Helen, 132
Cremation of Sam McGee, The, 68
Creative thinking activities, 38, 83, 98, 99, 115
Creative writing activities, 57, 66, 69–70, 85, 124–5
Crossing, The, 56

Dann, Michelle Me, 90
Destination Antarctica, 133
Dickinson, Emily
   clue questions, 25
   information sheet, 26
Dixon, Ann, 60
Dixon, Franklin W., 133
Dragon's Robe, The, 146

159

Economics activities, 66–67
Elaboration, 38–39, 126
Eldorado Adventure, The, 47–48
Ellis, Ella Thorp, 77
Environment (activities), 112, 113, 114, 134–6, 140
Equator, 80
Europe, 89–103
    activities, 95–103
    countries of, 92–94, 95
    maps of, 89, 95
    mnemonic story for, 92–94
    rivers of, 95, 96, 97
    suggested reading, 90–91
Expanding, sentences and phrases, 69

Fact or Fiction, 143–4
Falcon's Wing, The, 61
Farmer, Nancy, 107
Five Clue Game, 53–54, 101–2, 103
Flexibility, 38, 52, 124
Fluency, 38, 51, 124
Froman, Nan, 107

Garrigue, Sheila, 90
Geraghty, Paul, 106
Girl Named Disaster, A, 107
Global warming, 132
    activity, 140
Gold Coin, The, 47
Great Kapoc Tree, The, 76, 83
Great Lakes, 74
Greenfield, Eloise, 106
Greetings, Asia, 147
Griffiths, Helen, 77

Haida, 60, 64, 71
Hansen, Joyce, 107
Heartland, 3, 33
Hess, Paul, 47
Himalaya—Vanishing Cultures, 147
How Raven Brought Light to People, 60
Huckleberry Finn, 30
Hunter, The, 106

I Hear America Singing, 3, 34
I Sailed with Columbus, 3
Imagery, 141, 142
Imagination, 86, 87, 142

Important Book, The, 64
Indians, 60, 64, 71–73
Into the Mummy's Tomb, 107
Isabella's Bed, 76

Jacobs, Shannon K., 107
Jaguar, 77
Jaguar in the Rain Forest, 48
Johnson, Angela, 2
Journey of the Shadow Barns, The, 61

Land formations, U.S., 30–31
Larin, Anne, 146
Lattimore, Deborah Norse, 146
Lee, Cynthia, 147
Lee, Sandra Crow, 132
Lester, Alison, 76, 121
Literature activity (classics), 68
Lloyd, Alexander, 48
London, Jack, 68, 69
London, Jonathan, 61
Lowry, Lois, 91
Luba—The Angel of Bergen Belsen, 90
Lure activity, 153

MacDonald, Suse, 106
Map activities, 4, 80, 95, 137
Mathematics activity, 36. *See also* Computation
Metaphor activities, 69–70, 83–85
Mexico
    activities, 57–58
    map of, 46, 58
    suggested reading, 56
Mind mapping, 95
Mississippi, 3, 30
Mississippi River, 30, 33
Missouri, 28
Mnemonics
    goals and objectives, vii–viii
    rationale, vii–ix
    stories, 49, 62–63, 74, 78–79, 92–94, 108–110, 122–3, 130
Mojave, 3, 31
Morpurgo, Michael, 91

Nanta's Lion, 106
National Geography Standards, ix
Native Americans, 60, 64

Newton, Pam, 147
Nikola-Lisa, W., 2
Number the Stars, 91

Oberman, Sheldon, 90
Oceania
    map of 129
    mnemonic story about, 130
O'Dell, Scott, 56
Oregon Trail, 28, 29
Originality, 38

Panther Dream, A Story of the African Rainforest, 106
Parson, Nan, 61
Paulsen, Gary, 56
Penguin and Little Blue, 133
Penguins, 134, 135
Penguins and Polar Bears, 132
Perfect Crane, 146
Pigeon Hero, 90
Place puzzles activity, 5
Plants (activities), 53
Poetry activities, 30–31, 51
Pony Express, 28
Potlatch, 66
Prairie, 29
Problem-solving activities, 66, 113, 135, 136
Prompt activity, 153–4
Pumpkin Runner, The, 120

Quarters, commemorative, 36, 37, 38
Questioning and transfer, 98, 99
Quicksand Pony, The, 121
Quiz bowls, 53

Rain Forest Animals, 47
Rain forests, 50, 53
Recall activity, 112
Redmond, Shirley Raye, 90
Reeves, Nicholas, 107
Research activities, 50, 57, 64, 80, 96, 140
Reynolds, Jan, 147
Rhymes, 53, 153, 156
Rivers, 95, 96, 97
Roam the Wild Country, 77
Roth, Susan L., 120
Russian Federation, map of, 148
Ryder, Joanne, 47–48

Saguaro cactus, 31, 32, 39
Santa Fe Trail, 28, 29
Saturday Sancocho, 76
Sayre, April Pulley, 147
Schlein, Mirium, 3
Science activities, 53, 80, 126, 127–8
Senses, five, 127–8
Service, Robert, 68
Shelters, 155
Siebert, Diane, 3, 29, 30–31, 33
Sierra, 3, 30
Simile activities, 124–5, 142
Smith, Roland, 77
Socratic questioning, 100
Song of the Giraffe, 107
Sonoran Desert, 31
South America, 75–87
    activities, 80–87
    maps of, 75, 87
    mnemonic story about, 78–79
    suggested reading, 76–77
Spanish Language activity, 57
St. Louis Arch, 28
Stallion of the Sands, 77
Steps, The, 120
Stonecutter, The, 147
Stone Idol, The, 133
Story for a Black Night, 107
Sugaring-Off Party, The, 61
Survival (activities), 117, 118
Swan, Robert, 133
Synthesis, 116

Those Building Men, 2
Tillotson, Katherine, 133
"To Build a Fire," 68
Torres, Leyla, 76
Transfer, 98, 99
Treasure of Topo-El-Bampo, The, 56
Trees (activities), 50, 51, 81
Tropic of Cancer, 80
Tropic of Capricorn, 80
Tryszynska-Frederick, Luba, 90
Twain, Mark, 30

United States, 1–44
    activities, 4–44
    map clues, 40–43
    Midwestern states, 28

United States (Cont.)
   New England states, 25–27
   suggested reading, 2–3
   Western states, 29
U.S. Geography Standards, ix–x
U.S. Mint, 35, 36, 37

Very Last First Time, 60
Visualization, 153–4

Waiting for Anya, 91
Water (activities), 112, 113, 114

Way Home, The, 61
Webbing activities, 97
Weir, Bob, 106
Weir, Wendy, 106
Welcome to the Green House, 48
Westward Expansion, 28
White Fang, 68
Whitman, Walt, 3, 34

Yolen, Jane, 48

About the Author

JOAN EBBESMEYER is a retired teacher, now an adjunct professor at Missouri Baptist University in St. Louis, a storyteller, and a former Teacher Idea Press author (*Literature Lures*, 2002).

www.ingramcontent.com/pod-product-compliance
Lightning Source LLC
Chambersburg PA
CBHW080938300426
44115CB00017B/2870